DARKSIDE OF THE EARTH

SEX TRAFFICKING

JEFFSON NATHAN

Kindle Direct Publishing

Disclaimer

Case stories can cause melancholy and tears to sensitive readers. All images on the cover page and back are un-copyrighted taken from pexels.com. Each image depicts a meaning. The logos of the police and FBI depicts appreciation and respect for their ongoing support to 'counter sex trafficking', this includes integral law enforcement of all countries. The images of girls from diverse backgrounds are meant to respect them for being helpless victims or survivors and not stigmatized targets of negative speculations. The images of the accused and prisoners depict lawful conviction. All names of the victims and survivors used in the case stories are changed from the original, a few sentences of are added to make the stories more interesting. Any co-incidence of names used is unintentional and not subject to lawful dispute. Citations of information based on web reports are mentioned. Please note that all notes compiled in this book are meant for a good cause, for the purpose of edification and prevention of global crimes of sex trafficking.

For feedback and translation permission please mail to jeffsonn@gmail.com

CONTENTS

Acknowledgements

Coordinated efforts always lead to better results. I humbly express my gratitude to the organizations and individuals listed below, without whom this book would not be completed. Compliments to them and all other related organizations like CNN Freedom, International Justice Mission, Free a Girl, New Light, Shakti Vahini, and others [the list is long] for their ongoing challenging efforts to 'Counter Sex Trafficking' in various nations.

1. Mr. Manohar Waghela, founder - Transforming Lives Foundation
2. Mrs. Preeti Patkar, founder - PRERANA www.preranaantitrafficking.org
3. Mrs. Triveni Acharya, founder - Rescue Foundation www.rescuefoundation.net
4. Mr. Atul Aher, senior police inspector, New Mumbai Police
5. Mr. Raju Nepali, activist, founder - Duars Expressmail

Special thanks to The US State Department, UN Human Rights, Diplomats, Government ministers and bureaucrats. The officers of the judiciary and law enforcements in all nations cannot be forgotten, they all deserve a salute of appreciation for their integrity and efforts in prevention of the growth of Human Trafficking crimes.

Introduction

Just recently I remembered the title of the music album called 'Dark Side of the Moon.' It led me to create a title to this book.

Dark side of the Moon by the famous rock band Pink Floyd was released in the 70's! 'Us and Them' was a song title in this album....here's a sample of the lyrics and followed by part of its description according to Wikipedia:

'Us (us, us, us, us) and them (them, them, them, them)
And after all we're only ordinary men
Me
And you (you, you, you)
God only knows
It's not what we would choose (choose, choose) to do (to do, to do)'

Before I started working for the cause of rescuing slaves from sex trafficking, I was ignorant of the truth of trafficking. Some times as a teen, I would be riding with friends seated at the window seat in public transport buses in Mumbai, I would curiously see women standing outside the brothels on the streets. Little they knew, my friends would misinform me about them to be prostitutes or sinful people making money by doing the wrong things.

Actually they were and yet are, slaves exploited in order to earn for their bosses – the traffickers - pimps and brothel keepers.

This book follows my recently released book called 'Break Free from Stigmas of common mental disorders.' I realized that a high percentage of trafficked victims must be silent sufferers of combined mental health issues such as Depression; PTSD [post traumatic stress disorder]; Mood disorders; Borderline personality disorders; PPD [paranoid personality disorder] and Anxiety disorder. A majority, let's assume 95% must be affected by PTSD followed by depression. Information of the above disorders is explained in my book 'Break Free from Stigmas of CMD's' available on Amazon.

Persons are trafficked for commercial sexual exploitation, servitude, bondage, forced labor and other criminal purposes. 'Commercial Sexual Exploitation' is a better term for what is traditionally and conventionally, yet inaccurately, referred to as prostitution. The term Commercial Sexual Exploitation indicates 'exploitation' as an essential characteristic of the transaction. The word 'commercial' in it indicates the commoditization of a human being. As an organization working with victims of trafficking for commercial sexual exploitation, we have come across cases that appear in the media as cases of sex trafficking but turn out to be cases of migration fraud or smuggling – Prerana

In India, the city of Kolkata (Calcutta) has the largest commercial sex market followed by Delhi and Mumbai as the second largest. In the years 2011-12 and 2015, I had the opportunity to work in an organization called 'Transforming Lives Foundation.' We did surveillance of forced victims and minor victims of sex trafficking in the commercial capital of India called Mumbai (Bombay). I was glad to be part of many rescue operations of female victims [some of them minor virgins] in effective coordination with Mumbai and Thane senior police officers and their teams.

My last mission in January 2022 was as an undercover volunteer sent to trap one trafficker [in a north eastern city] and lead him to a meeting with five other big time traffickers in another eastern city. I took him by a short flight after treating him with good booze and a happy meal! From the arrival airport we were followed by undercover cops ready to cast the net on the other five at the preplanned meeting spot. It was a big success. Smiling to myself, I walked away with thoughts of victory towards a waiting taxi after the net was cast on them. The taxi took me to the main station where I had to board a train back. At the station I had to return the special mobile phone to the uniformed officer waiting for me. He handed over a box of special deserts [a tradition to celebrate] and expressed his respect and gratitude verbally and saluted me for the special mission accomplished. Details of this story are confidential as the case is subjudice. About 82 slaves including minors were held by those fugitives awaiting their placements and transportation.

During my experience of anti human trafficking, I gathered maximum knowledge from my boss, my female colleagues, co-operative police officers and from police events related to sex trafficking. Soon after I left the NGO to travel to Canada, I wrote an article on 'Awareness of Sex Trafficking' meant to educate girls and young women. This can be read in the second last chapter of this book.

It is also uploaded on medium. The link below may be shared on social media platforms

Awareness of Sex Trafficking. Edification of girls on awareness of… | by Jeffson Nathan | Medium

Besides this, I have uploaded a video in slow and simple English on You Tube explaining points of prevention meant to be followed by girls and young women in the world. Please share the link on social media, like and subscribe for related posts in future. Since this is an awareness initiative, I encourage anyone to feel free to translate these points in local or state languages and share it with those who don't understand English. You Tube link of the video:

https://www.youtube.com/watch?
v=SazZMIcxcws&ab_channel=JeffsonNathan

I encourage readers to help translate such awareness in other languages and share it as much as possible.

The thought of writing this book was in the pipeline for some years. It has now become possible with the support of 'Transforming Lives Foundation.' From the third chapter onwards I have compiled specific true case histories narrated by survivors to my female colleagues and contributed by my friendly partners in anti sex trafficking, rescue and rehabilitation causes.

The purpose of this book is to mainly educate girls, young women and all women globally. It is meant to initiate measures to break the customer demand. It is also meant to edify parents, men and professionals so that the awareness to prevent sex trafficking is encouraged and spread out via social media. This is one easy way we can avoid the vulnerable from falling into traps of traffickers.

Some notes in the first two chapters are taken from reliable websites that are cited within meant for the purpose of edification and prevention.

For feedback and permission to translate please mail me: jeffsonn@gmail.com

You may also communicate via Facebook messenger, Twitter DM and Instagram

What's Dark about Global Sex Trafficking?

It's a product of evil. It's an inhumane criminal activity worse than drug trafficking. It's a worldwide menace to young girls and women. It's rightfully called growing modern times slavery. It involves immense stages of mental and physical suffering caused to helpless, harmless and defenseless innocents. Appropriate to fit its definition is the biblical verse from John 10:10…The devil [thief, enemy] comes to steal, to kill and to destroy.

'Modern slavery is a serious and high harm crime in which people are treated as commodities, bought, sold, and exploited for criminal gain. The term modern slavery encompasses two criminal offences: human trafficking; and slavery, servitude and forced or compulsory labor. Preventing modern slavery
is vitally important to reduce the long-term impacts of the crime and safeguard vulnerable individuals from harm' – excerpted from UNSEEN report UK

The life long journey of darkness for the victim begins as soon as she shockingly realizes the fact that she has been deceived. Trafficking happens almost everywhere in the world….not just in rural suburbs and villages. City girls are still reported missing every day with little chances of finding them.

In a post war zone survivors are struck with poverty to the extremes; war causes desperation and desolation. Basic needs of medicine, food, shelter, etc. are affected.

There's a profound sense of uncertainty and emptiness among the mentally traumatized survivors overwhelmed at what they have already experienced. Sadly, a post war zone is a potential area to catch many fish into one net. Human traffickers must be eagerly lurking with strategies to cast their nets in Ukraine now [at the time of this writing.] They have successfully done so in Syria, Iraq and Bosnia-Serbia in the last few decades. Women in Afghanistan are not spared either. Most cases are unreported; however, since sex trafficking existed in the past, it is expected to be prevalent in the present when living conditions have dropped extremely low.

https://en.wikipedia.org/wiki/
Human_trafficking_in_Afghanistan#:~:text=In
%202008%2C%20the%20Afghan%20government,bans
%20and%20punishes%20Baja%2DBazi.

In sex trafficking, inducing a sense of immense coercive fear in the victim's mind by means of loud tones of verbal abuses, threats, blackmail [to comply or else siblings will be killed], severe physical abuses [burns and cuts] and starvation are the first steps of atrocities caused to the victim to be submissive. This happens in the first few days before the first incident of sexual abuse which defines a criminal offence of rape. The victim is mentally traumatized especially if she is a minor she is subject to forceful and painful breaking of her hymen. This first phase of suffering is bound to cause PTSD [post traumatic stress disorder] and Depression to all victims of sex slavery. Paranoia may follow closely to some of them in the second phase.

Trauma is any experience that overwhelms our ability

to cope and undermines our sense of safety. Trauma can inspire powerlessness and hopelessness relative to our capacity to defend ourselves. It can rob us of the belief in our ability to heal, trust, live, and love as we once did, before the traumatic experience occurred. Experiences of trauma can lead to trauma-related disorders, such as post-traumatic stress disorder or PTSD. Trauma can be collective (experienced by a group of persons) or individual (experienced by one). It can be episodic (happening every so often), isolated (happening once), or chronic (unabating). It can even be vicarious (e.g. by empathically engaging with the trauma of others. - Katherine Schreiber – Psychology Today

This darkness that gets even darker and darker for the victim is unimaginable and yet sidelined as a non prioritized subject by governments of most countries.

Human Trafficking is an organized crime which may be operated under the leadership of a politician of a mafia kingpin. Globally, its growth has not stopped. It involves a network of criminals and commonly corrupt underpaid junior staff among police and border security guards. Human Trafficking is split into to two main divisions - one for selling victims for forced labor, begging, illegal organ sales and the other for sexual exploitation. In this book my focus is on sex trafficking for the purpose of edification and prevention. Websites, dating Apps and social media communications are an effective way to lure girls into trafficking similarly the same platforms can be used to educate girls and counter trafficking. It can be effective now that everyone's focused on their phones.

Traffickers abusing online technology, UN crime prevention agency warns
https://news.un.org/en/story/2021/10/1104392

Human Trafficking and Social Media
https://polarisproject.org/human-trafficking-and-social-media/

Every victim caught up in a trafficker's casting net has a clear and identifiable vulnerability that the trafficker has used to conduct surveillance of the victim. In case of child victims the most identified vulnerability is poverty and the targets are the prospective parents most of who are used by acquaintances such as friends or relatives or referrals. Child victims, also referred to as minors below 18 years of age are most vulnerable as they are easier to convince and less rebellious. The four methods of trafficking minors are listed below.

1. Family betrayal: Through immediate family members manipulating and selling them for various reasons.
2. Survival sex: When the victim doesn't have a seller but a direct buyer who wishes to keep her as a full time or part time live in partner and pays for services. Though there is no coercion and enslavement here, the buyer can be charged if the victim is a minor. Survival sex is mostly done by the agreement of the victim who could be brain washed. It's more common in western cultures where 'live in' relationships are culturally acceptable.
3. Gang controlled: Gangs and mafia groups who indulge in various criminal activities and operate with weapons 24/7.One member of the gang uses tactics to start a romantic relationship and grooming method to

eventually induce the victim as a full time commodity for gang members. This method is common in Latin America, USA and some parts of Europe.

4. Pimp controlled: This method is most common globally as the pimp or agent [who could be anyone familiar] as the first trafficker to lure, transport and sell the victim. In some incidences the victim is kidnapped from an outdoor spot by a deceptive approach usually done by sweet talking strangers who are mostly women.

Most enslaved persons have been trapped by someone they knew. Innocents bound to get enslaved were not always engaged in promiscuous behavior or risky activities. Often they were involved in associating with a friend they thought they could trust. Online chatting on Facebook and various other online sources are commonly used to lure teens and immature youth with impressive videos and images. Globally it is believed that it is easier to lure teens. The younger they are, the more responsive they are to submit to fearful behavior administered to them. In developing countries rural poverty is a potential fertile ground for traffickers to operate. When people's income is affected due loss or unemployment, war or recent migration, they fall under criminal's surveillance. Most criminals conduct days or weeks of surveillance on targets. Some traffickers disguise themselves as employment agents to those in need of a job. Some traffickers can be well groomed, well mannered and equipped with impressive jewelry, gadgets or vehicles.

They can display a lot of pretense in the way they speak and behave. In the cities, they are known to lure the vulnerable to expensive restaurants in swank cars. Traffickers have been and still can be women to lure young girls. They can use various techniques of pretense - to pass off as a married couple for example.

Sex slavery is more rampant now than it has ever been. The market demand and networking of sex trafficking occupies 79% of all human trafficking cases in the world. Traffickers have taken advantage of lockdowns during the pandemic. Many of those affected due to the loss of income during lockdowns especially in rural parts of the world were targeted by traffickers. A look at the globe shows us the high number of underdeveloped countries in the continents of Asia, Africa, Europe and South America that were under the radar of traffickers. While transportation was limited to essential services in the lockdowns, the preparatory phases of keeping victims ready were completed with the easy and effective means of social media communications.

*One of the most entrenched forms of organized violence against women is sex trafficking which is defined as the following stages:

·	Recruitment [usually done by a familiar acquaintance, family friend or relative]
·	Transportation [from village to town, to city, to state and/or even to another country]
·	Transfer [resale post sexual exploitation from one source to another potential buyer]
·	Harboring or receipt of persons by means of threat or use of force or other forms of coercion, of abduction, of fraud, of deception, of the abuse of power or of a

position of vulnerability or of the giving or receiving of payments or benefits to achieve the consent of a person having control over another person, for the purpose of exploitation according to the *United Nations report 2000

The United Nations Office on Drugs and Crime (UNODC) global report (UN 2018) stated that over 70% of trafficked victims were female and underwent sexual exploitation.

*The trafficking of women and children for sexual exploitation is the fastest growing criminal enterprise in the world. This profitable industry generates an estimated $99 billion each year. Unsurprisingly, women and girls make up 96 percent of victims of sex trafficking. The action of sexual exploitation is a clear human rights violation. This exploitation robs these women and girls of integrity, dignity, health, security and equality [*U.S. Department of State report 2020]

'Soft Targets' of traffickers to prey upon are:

·   The poverty stricken and the ones who are desperate to earn a living by
        legal means

·   The innocent teens vulnerable to get easily influenced to move to greener
        pastures

·   The immature youth involved in habitual use of intoxicants most
        commonly being alcohol and marijuana

·   The ones who are promiscuous by character

·   The ones struggling with mental health issues and

disorders that

causes them to be sexually hyperactive

·   The ones who frequently visit areas of sexual pleasure such as adult

entertainment clubs

·   The immature or innocent ones who have run away from home to escape

forms of family originated abuse or extreme poverty conditions

·   The ones who are in unstable means of housing especially in areas

affected by natural disasters or war

·   The ones who have recently migrated to a new place and are seeking

opportunities to settle down. The ones who have suddenly lost their

parents due to a natural disaster or an accident

The primary master trapper motivated by hardened criminals could be:

·   Intimate partners [trusted boyfriends, partners or even husbands]
·   Family members [could be uncles, aunts, step/real fathers or shockingly

even mothers]
·   Others [relatives, strangers in disguise who approach to help, armed

criminals, unarmed kidnappers]
·   Friends or referrals of a trusted friend or relative of the victim

Possible destination of victims depending on the market demand

- Brothels
- Private apartments/villas/bungalows/houses
- Illegal clubs/orgy parties
- Nude dance bars
- Illicit adult entertainment businesses such as strip clubs
- Escort services
- Private services to business travelers in hotels, motels and lodges
- Pornography production studios
- Illicit massage/spa businesses

According to the UNODC report, the most common form of human trafficking (79%) is sexual exploitation. The victims of sexual exploitation are predominantly women and girls. Surprisingly, in 30% of the countries which provided information on the gender of traffickers, women make up the largest proportion of traffickers. In some parts of the world, women trafficking women is the norm.

https://www.unodc.org/unodc/en/human-trafficking/global-report-on-trafficking-in-persons.html

Psychiatric and Somatic ailments victims are prone to

Health care professionals will agree here. Individuals who experience abuse or trauma especially during their growth years are highly prone to be affected with psychiatric or somatic issues. Listed below are some of the ailments most victims may silently suffer from during captivity:

Psychiatric related

- Depression
- PTSD [post traumatic stress disorder]
- Mood disorders
- Borderline personality disorders
- PPD [paranoid personality disorder]
- Anxiety disorder

Somatic related

- Scars caused due to external injuries [burns and cuts]
- Poor growth and low immunity caused due to malnourishment
- Gynecological complications
- Gastroenterological complications due to improper diet
- Sexually transmitted diseases [gonorrhea and syphilis]
- HIV and AIDS

In cases of severe somatic affliction caused to the captivated due to infections, blood loss, dehydration, drug overdose or disease - hospitalization is avoided. The victim is left to die or is killed and secretly disposed. You may come across such actual and shocking scenarios in some of the movies on sex trafficking. We've heard and read news reports of boats capsized in the sea drowning many victims of human trafficking seeking asylum in other countries. Such incidences are allegedly made to happen. Criminals are mercilessly violent especially when they are intoxicated with drugs like cocaine. The devil comes to steal, kill and destroy.

Readers are encouraged to read a well researched report on sex trafficking during the last two years of the pandemic available at the following link.

https://www.globenewswire.com/news-release/2022/02/09/2382047/0/en/BedBible-com-Reports-on-2022-Worldwide-Sex-Trafficking-Statistics.html

All notes onwards are according to the above report - There have never been so many child victims. Worldwide, almost 20% of all victims are children. However, in some parts of Africa and the Mekong region, children are the majority (up to 100%).

The significant part of the victims of sex trafficking come from East Europe (Ukraine, Belarus, Moldavia and Romania); Asia (Burma, Thailand, Cambodia, Vietnam, and The Philippines); West Africa (Nigeria, Cameroon, Ivory Coast, and Sierra Leona) and Middle America (Mexico, Colombia, Honduras, Guatemala and Jamaica)

The areas where sexual exploitation is taking place are countries in North and West Europe together with USA and Asia as leading areas. Especially countries like Poland, Turkey, The Philippines, Thailand, Cambodia, United Arab Emirates, USA and Argentina.

Northern America [USA, Canada and Greenland]
The overall average of adult victims is 70% and minor victims is 30%

Central America [Mexico, Guatemala, Honduras, Nicaragua, Costa Rica, Panama, Cuba, and the Caribbean islands]

Adult victims = 52% and minor victims = 48%

South America [Argentine, Brazil, Uruguay, Paraguay, Bolivia, Peru, Ecuador, Colombia, Venezuela, Guyana, and Surinam]
Adult victims = 73% and minor victims = 27%

Northern Europe [Norway, Denmark, Sweden, Finland, Great Britain, Iceland, Estonia, Latvia, and Lithuania]
Adult victims = 94% and minor victims = 6%

Western Europe [France, Germany, Belgium, Austria, Switzerland, Netherland, Luxembourg, and Monaco]
Adult victims = 94% and minor victims = 6%

Eastern Europe [Russia, Poland, Ukraine, Romania, Bulgaria, Belarus, Hungary, Czech Republic, and Slovakia]
Adult victims = 92% and minor victims = 8%

Southern Europe [Portugal, Spain, Italy, Croatia, Serbia, Greece, Albania, Macedonia, Kosovo, and Montenegro]
Adult victims = 89% and minor victims = 11%

Northern Africa [Morocco, Algeria, Tunisia, Western Sahara, Libya, Egypt, and Sudan]
Like most regions the majority is adult victims

Central Africa
Cameroon, Central African Republic, Chad, Congo Republic – Brazzaville, Democratic Republic of Congo, Equatorial Guinea, Gabon, and São Tomé & Principe. More interesting is that out of all cases child sex trafficking happens for 47%. That's a really big portion and the biggest in all regions of the world.

Western Africa

Benin, Burkina Faso, Cape Verde, Côte D'Ivoire, Gambia, Ghana, Guinea, Guinea-Bissau, Liberia, Mali, Mauritania, Niger, Nigeria, Senegal, Sierra Leone, and Togo. Like Middle Africa, it has relatively many child victims compared to the rest of the world.

Eastern Africa
Burundi, Comoros, Djibouti, Eritrea, Ethiopia, Kenya, Madagascar, Malawi, Mauritius, Réunion, Rwanda, Seychelles, Somalia, Somaliland, Tanzania, and Uganda. Looking further into the age we find that the 9-17 years old are the age group with most identified victims. This region also has a high amount of child sex trafficking cases.

Southern Africa
As regards the age breakdown and majority distribution it's quite similar to Northern Africa.

Western Asia
Bahrain, Iraq, Jordan, Kuwait, Lebanon, Oman, State of Palestine, Qatar, Saudi Arabia, Syrian Arab Republic, United Arab Emirates, and Yemen
Adult victims = 97% and minor victims = 3%

Central Asia
Kazakhstan, Kyrgyz Republic, Tajikistan, Turkmenistan, and Uzbekistan
It has like the European regions almost an equal-weighted distribution between female and male cases (51% to 49%)

Southern Asia
Bangladesh, Bhutan, India, Pakistan, Nepal, Sri Lanka, and Afghanistan

1.02% of the sex trafficking victims happen in this region. 58% are females and 42% are males. More interesting is that almost 41% of the victims are between 9-17 years old with adult victims = 53% and minor victims = 47% with the age group between 18-20 at 11%; 21-23 at 7%; 24-26 at 6%; 27-29 at 6% and 30-38 at 14%

Eastern Asia
China, Hong Kong, Japan, Macau, Mongolia, North Korea, South Korea, and Taiwan; Compared to Southern Asia there are not many child victims.

Southern-Eastern Asia
Adult victims = 82% and minor victims = 18%

Australia and New Zealand
Australia and New Zealand are recognized for their less than 0.5% victims and the fact that it's the only region with more male victims (91%) than female victims (9%). And lastly, it has only adult cases.

Africa and Southern Asia has many child sex trafficking cases (Around 50% of all cases is with minors)

Over 50% of the worlds sex trafficking happens in the USA.
Females are more frequently a victim in sex trafficking than men.

Sex trafficking in the USA

A survivor in a You Tube video mentioned that there is not a single town in every state of the nation that is not affected by sex trafficking! The USA is the country where most of the trafficking takes place in the world with Texas and California reported to have the highest number of cases.

Sex trafficking is an profitable business (Exclusive insights)

The average annual profit for every woman in sex trafficking is $ 100.000. The average for both genders is $ 21.800. Further, the report reveals that sexual exploitation can yield a return on investment ranging from 100% to 1,000%. In the Netherlands, investigators were able to calculate the profit generated by two sex traffickers from a number of victims. One trafficker earned $ 18,148 per month from four victims (for a total of $ 127,036) while the second trafficker earned $ 295,786 in the 14 months that three women were sexually exploited.

The pandemic impact

During the lockdowns, as the proportion of victims from common recruitment sites such as strip clubs (-46%), foster homes (-70%), and schools (-38%) went down drastically, the internet was reported as the top recruitment location for all forms of trafficking. Most notably, the analysis found a significant increase in the proportion of potential victims for whom Facebook and Instagram were the sites for recruitment into trafficking (120%). 125% increase in reports of recruitment on Facebook over the previous year. 95% increase in reports of recruitment on Instagram over the previous year.

Experts are afraid that the pandemic has increased the number of sex trafficking cases/victims. It seems like the organizers have been more direct in their communication to the victims. This is due to the increased challenges that the pandemic has given rise to.

"Trafficking in Texas has risen during the COVID-19 pandemic. That's because economic problems caused by the pandemic have made the problem of human trafficking worse" – Samantha Hernandez, Mobilization Director for Elijah Rising

"The pandemic has increased vulnerabilities to trafficking in persons while making trafficking even harder to detect and leaving victims struggling to obtain help and access to justice" - Ghada Waly, Executive Director UNODC

The other side of
Darkness in India

Since decades, India is a source of one of its biggest criminal activities; it is a destination and transit country for men, women and children trafficked into forced labor and sexual exploitation. It has easily accessible land borders with Nepal, Bhutan, Myanmar [Burma] and Bangladesh. Borders of Pakistan, China and Tibet have difficult terrain and high security. Sex trafficking is supposedly one of the largest criminal activities in India with many cases that remain unreported. The diversity of oversized populations, easier geographical access, easier means of transportation, corrupt elements, poverty, lack of rural literacy and greater urban market demand are the combined advantages for external and internal sex trafficking in India to prosper. Most accused traffickers manage to get bailed out from prison sentences. Most get back to the trafficking business making it a harder challenge for honest police officers and NGO workers.

According to some estimates, the annual turnover in India is around INR 20 billion (approx. US$ 412mn). Although there are no official numbers, the United Nations Office on Drugs and Crime (UNODC) estimates that 150,000 people are trafficked in South Asia every year.

90% of trafficking in India is internal, and those from India's most disadvantaged social economic strata including the lowest castes are particularly vulnerable to forced or bonded labor and sex trafficking. The most vulnerable amongst these are women and children who are trafficked for the purposes of forced prostitution.

Since 2004, India has been in the Tier 2 category of US Governments Watch List for Human Trafficking.

Although the government of India does not fully comply with the minimum standards for the elimination of trafficking, it is making significant efforts to do so.

There are no official records for the numbers of women and children working in prostitution but estimates make harrowing reading with some saying that between 300,000 and 500,000 prostitutes in India are children – i.e. 40% of the industry.

Trafficking is a complex issue and requires a multifaceted approach. Nonprofits have emerged in the last few years that look at various interventions along the chain of prevention, protection and prosecution. Some work in source areas, some work in destination areas, some work in rescue, some work in rehabilitation, others focus on seeking to work with the government to change policy.

As you will go on to read, Prerana is a leader in India in this space and has at the forefront of efforts that culminated in the 2011 Supreme Court observation that observed: "The word "life" in Article 21 of the Constitution of India has been interpreted in several decisions of this court to mean a right to "life with dignity". It is only if a sex worker is able to earn a livelihood through technical skills rather than by selling her body that she can live with dignity, and that is why we have requested all the States and the Union of India to submit schemes for giving technical training to these sex workers." – www.preranaantitrafficking.org

According to the Global Slavery Index 2018, published by the Australia-based human rights group called 'The Walk Free Foundation,' on any given day in 2016 there were nearly 8 million people living in 'modern slavery' in India. We are now in 2022! Modern slavery covers a set of specific legal concepts like forced labor, debt bondage, forced marriage, slavery and slavery-like practices; as well as human trafficking which refers to situations of exploitation that 'a person cannot refuse or leave because of threats, violence, coercion, deception, and abuse of power.'

With its current population of more than a billion, India is the second largest country in the world. However, with its size comes a mountain of human rights issues. Many of the vulnerable ignorant innocents can easily fall under the radar of traffickers amidst such an oversized population. India is a hub of one of the most prominent human rights issues; unfortunately the system doesn't yet pay much attention to bring human trafficking under control. Widespread corruption among low key authorities and low rank law enforcement personnel feeds the greedy network of organized crime to continue.

The investment costs involved in trafficking victims is less while the income is not just high, it's a recurring source of income. This is a global fact. Criminal networks can be slippery. Just as everybody else, they are now tech savvy with communications with a choice of social media platforms and apps available. They're advanced at maintaining one step forward of the under equipped law personnel with smarter ploys. Many are equipped with modern gadgets and technology such as encrypted communication channels to outwit authorities. The lockdowns have only made their task easier as the understaffed and under equipped police forces are usually caught up in between to prioritize diverse issues of the overpopulated people. Here we have noted that even honest officers are overburdened and helpless at times to be submissive to authorities and sometimes politicians. Unscheduled demands of protection during movements of small time fussy politicians have to be fulfilled by the stressed out police personnel.

Trust foundations or non government organizations [NGO's] in India struggle with financial funding. In recent years the government abruptly stopped the renewal of foreign funding licenses [FCRA] for all NGOs, some of which have head offices abroad and are involved in doing great humanitarian work. Many NGOs, including church organizations were affected by FCRA blockings; some of them had to shut operations. The Missionaries of Charity which is Mother Theresa's foundation fought for their rights that caused the government to flip.

In India, kidnappings for labor and sexual needs have been constant. In spite of many genuine efforts, the country remains hindered by its inadequate solutions to alleviate the problem and the department feels that India did not sufficiently ensure the mitigation of the issue.

"The pandemic has increased vulnerabilities to trafficking in persons while making trafficking even harder to detect and leaving victims struggling to obtain help and access to justice" - Ghada Waly, Executive Director UNODC

Victims of sex trafficking in India are predominantly the young illiterate girls from impoverished families in rural states. Pandemic lockdowns in the last two years have increased poverty rates and the downfall of the economy has made the poor poorer and the traffickers greedier at the same time. Sex trafficking in India continues to be a lucrative business and is persistent since decades. It has been on an escalation. Many vulnerable women and girls are lured into the commercial sex industry because of the brain washing promises made of employment and dreams of getting rich in a short period of time. When these rural women and girls are faced with the harsh reality of poverty, hunger and homelessness many of them see this as the only option. Matters of poverty are sometimes so severe that parents will sell their own daughters into the trade. These women and children have no other options to depend on because they do not possess basic education, skills or resources to escape from sex slavery. In India families who hope for better prospects for their children are often targeted by traffickers posing as agents, who promise the family a good home or schooling for their child. The families are ignorant of what would happen to their child forced into slavery, many families have no clue or news about their daughters. Poor illiterate communities are especially vulnerable to human traffickers, with limited opportunities to make money, the rosy picture of good offers are hard to decline for young women.

The fact that around 174 minors go missing every day in India, and only half are ever found, is proof enough that current arrangements from the government are inadequate. The system to fight human trafficking in India is way backward which gives an upper hand to the networking of criminals. The conditions of the government run shelter homes for rescued victims are pathetic. There's always been a shortage of space to admit new victims. Some of them are turned back and courts are forced to set them free causing the traffickers to trap them back into the trade.

Efforts to audit government run or funded shelters remained inadequate, and significant shortcomings in protections for victims, especially children, remain unaddressed. Many victims waited years to receive central government mandated compensation, and often state and district legal offices did not proactively request the compensation or assist victims in filing applications. Some foreign trafficking victims remained in state-run shelters for years due to lengthy or non-existent repatriation processes.

Additionally, the government prosecuted sex trafficking crimes under other laws like the Protection of Children from Sexual Offenses Act (POCSO) and the Immoral Trafficking Prevention Act (ITPA), which criminalized various offenses relating to commercial sexual exploitation. POCSO is non bailable while ITPA is bailable. The recruitment of children younger than age 18 by non-state armed groups is criminally prohibited by Section 83 (1) of the Juvenile Justice Act. A draft anti-trafficking bill from 2018 lapsed with the dissolution of the lower house in 2019. The government was working on a revised bill, which was yet to be presented to Parliament at the close of the reporting period.

Government-run and -funded shelters remained insufficient, facing serious shortages of space, financial resources, and trained personnel. NGOs relied primarily on donor contributions, although some received government funds. The disbursal of government funding to NGOs was sometimes delayed for multiple years. In 2020, an amendment to the Foreign Contribution Regulation Act that prevented the sub-granting of foreign contributions from the original Indian NGO recipient to other NGOs came into force, preventing collaboration and coordination and severely affecting their activities, including anti-trafficking NGOs.

Media, NGOs, and authorities continued to document a lack of oversight and negligence in government-run, government-funded, and privately run shelters that sometimes resulted in abuse and trafficking of residents. In several cases, such homes continued to operate despite significant gaps in mandatory reporting and allegations of abuse, at times due to alleged political connections. Child Welfare Committees [CWC] were designed to routinely monitor victim shelters and provide updates on victims' cases, although their efficacy varied across states. CWCs promoted interagency collaboration to prevent trafficking during the pandemic.

Foreign victims had the same access to shelter and services as Indian nationals. Government policy on foreign victims dictated their return to their country of origin at the earliest possible time. Authorities detained foreign sex trafficking victims in shelters until deportation, and both repatriation of foreign victims seeking to return home and deportation of victims could take years due to bureaucratic constraints. In July 2020, a group of Nepali trafficking victims were stranded in a Manipur shelter due to a lack of clear procedures to facilitate their repatriation. Some officials refused to repatriate victims until they had provided testimony in prosecutions against their traffickers. The government continued to review its 2015 memorandum of understanding with the Government of Bangladesh on identification and repatriation of Bangladeshi trafficking victims. The lengthy and complex approval system forced some Bangladeshi victims to languish in Indian shelters for years before repatriation. Media reported 180 Bangladeshi sex trafficking victims were awaiting repatriation at various shelters in West Bengal, many of whom have waited years for the conclusion of the 15-step approval process.

Traffickers exploit millions of people in commercial sex within India. Scheduled caste females were sometimes exploited through the traditional 'Jogini' system, in which Dalit [lower caste] women and girls are ceremoniously "married" to a local temple deity but in practice are used as sex slaves for higher caste villagers. Traffickers target Indian women and girls, but also fraudulently recruit significant numbers of Nepali and Bangladeshi women and girls to India for sex trafficking. Additionally, traffickers exploit women and girls from Central Asian, European, and African countries in commercial sex, especially in the state of Goa. NGOs reported that internal trafficking victims in western India came from almost every state. In addition to traditional red light districts, dance bars, spas, and massage parlors, traffickers increasingly exploit women and children in sex trafficking in hotels, lodges, guest houses, vehicles, huts, and private clubs and residences. Media outlets report the recruitment of women and children for commercial sex increasingly took place through social media platforms, including mobile dating applications and websites. Traffickers use encrypted digital communication applications to conduct transactions, enabling them to evade law enforcement. In addition, traffickers increasingly utilize digital payment applications in place of cash to evade suspicion. India is a source for child sex tourists and a destination for child sex tourism.

Traffickers kidnap and force Indian and Nepali women

and girls to work as "orchestra dancers" in India, especially in Bihar state, where girls perform with dance groups until they have repaid fabricated debts. Traffickers exploit women and children in sex trafficking in religious pilgrimage centers and in tourist destinations. Some traffickers kidnap children from public places, including railway stations, entice girls with drugs, and force girls as young as 5 years old in sex trafficking to take hormone injections to appear older. Some law enforcement officers protect suspected traffickers and brothel owners from law enforcement efforts and take bribes from sex trafficking establishments and sexual services from victims. According to one report, police have accepted bribes to release child sex trafficking victims back into traffickers' custody. Traffickers arrange sham marriages within India and Gulf states to subject females to sex trafficking. There have been isolated reports of physical and sexual abuse in some government, NGO and privately run shelter homes, including of trafficking victims, and compelling shelter residents into forced labor and sex trafficking in previous reporting periods.

Traffickers force many Indian migrants who willingly seek employment abroad into construction, domestic work, factories, and other low-skilled sectors in many regions, especially Gulf countries and Malaysia, often following recruitment fraud and exorbitant recruitment fees. Indian female domestic workers in Gulf countries, particularly Kuwait and Saudi Arabia, consistently report strong indicators of forced labor, including non-payment of wages, physical abuse and refusal to allow workers to leave upon completion of their contracts.

India is a global hotspot for child sex trafficking. Yet, the commercial sexual exploitation of children thrives in many rural Indian villages, fueled by a wide caste discrimination, family tradition, and poverty. In response, this study aimed to investigate minor sex trafficking among a particular culturally unique and geographically isolated population, in relation to the dominant human trafficking literature. In-depth interviews were conducted with 31 female members of the Bedia caste - a unique population whose primary form of income is derived from participation in the rural sex trade. It's a community tradition.

For women and girls who experience trafficking, it's an experience that often stays with them for the rest of their lives, a scar that can hold them back from education and employment opportunities. The stigma is deep and the trend is increasing, according to Reuters.

According to the website of School for Justice, there are an estimated 1.2 million under aged girls working in brothels in India alone, the highest number in the world, but in 2015 there were only 55 convictions for sex trafficking. It was this culture of impunity that led Hölsken to found the School for Justice. "In India, people involved in child prostitution, including traffickers, brothel owners, pimps and customers are rarely punished," Hölsken wrote in an email. "To put an end to this injustice and to take the offenders off the streets, we launched the School for Justice."

Abuse before being Trafficked

To induce coercive fear as compliance methods, sex trafficked victims invariably get physically and sexually abused, directly or indirectly by their traffickers and customers continuously before being trafficked, while being trafficked and/or after being trafficked too.

Majority of the survivors underwent long-term sexual abuse by family members or relatives when they were very young. According to 'Task Force on Trafficking of Women and Girls' studies, this would have made the survivor feel pervasively helpless and therefore lacking hope to be able to fight against injustice. The younger the abused are, the larger the duration of abuse, the tougher the recovery. In the present study, it was found that 43 out of 51 participants were victims of verbal abuse, physical abuse, or sexual abuse by parents, relatives, friends, siblings and/or strangers. They reported having been very upset due to the abuse they were undergoing, and that the trafficker presented themselves as concerned well-wishers, which made them appear trustworthy.

Task Force on Trafficking of Women and Girls identified the following range of reactions among the sex trafficked: fear, guilt, rage, sense of betrayal, distrust, helplessness, shock, suspicion and feeling of being lost. The sex trafficked women suffer from depression, self-blame guilt, anger and sleep disturbances. They are commoditized and lose their self-esteem and the capability to trust, leading them to psychological problems, since traffickers use the most effective and irresistible physical and psychological forms of abuse and psychological coercion to convince the victims to trust them.

Sex trafficking inevitably includes violence. The women who were silent while being sex trafficked were ill-treated and abused by husbands, in-laws and significant others, prior to being sex trafficked.

Please note that some parts of the information above are compiled from the following websites:

https://www.state.gov/reports/2021-trafficking-in-persons-report/india/

https://borgenproject.org/tag/human-trafficking-in-india/

https://journals.sagepub.com/doi/full/10.1177/09737030211003657

https://pubmed.ncbi.nlm.nih.gov/35156452/

The Indian Lockdown Effect

The plight of migrants in India's first lockdown

So called 'Migrants' were daily wage laborers in bigger cities who had started an exodus towards their villages in the Eastern and North Eastern parts of India during the first lockdown.

One of India's top journalists Barkha Dutt covered the entire first lockdown in India on the road reporting along with her team. They dared various kinds of challenges and the vulnerabilities of getting infected.

According to Vir Sanghvi, journalist and author, "she made the mainstream media focus on the human tragedies of Covid and especially on the entirely avoidable tragedy that was the migrants' exodus caused by a hastily imposed, ill-conceived lockdown. Her reports had a gritty authenticity and as thousands watched them on their phones and computers, the mainstream media narrative finally changed."

They walked under the blazing sun and through desolate, dark, moonless nights, sometimes barefoot and sometimes wearing flip-flop slippers made from rubber, their entire universe tied into small sacks carried aloft on their shoulders, holding on to the last packet of glucose biscuits and water before those too ran out. The women carried the physical belongings, stuffed usually into a makeshift carry bag knotted from a spare sari; the men carried their toddlers on their backs - Barkha Dutt in her recently released on book called 'To hell and back: humans of Covid'

For better understanding of the migrant's story, you could also access reports available on the internet; this is one of them:

https://www.bbc.com/news/world-asia-india-52672764

Now, here's the information untold by the media, I got from one of my colleagues who covers the North Eastern part of India with dedication and in depth work to counter sex trafficking.

Before the exodus, many migrants were already slaves of labor exploitation in the northern states of Haryana and Punjab. Some of them were domestic workers to Delhi's upper class residents. These daily wage workers besides others depending on daily wages were suddenly affected by the sudden imposition of the lockdown. Migrants were forced to leave as their employers panicked of fear. Sex slaves were told to leave the brothels. Since most of them were illiterate, their tolerance capability was low to handle that sudden tsunami that hit them. Holding on to their basic bundles of clothing, they feared getting infected and dying. On the exodus they suffered from disorientation and memory loss due to sudden high levels of stress. Most remembered their own names and the destination they were headed to. There was constant fear, panic and worry of reaching their destinations. They barely had money, clothing, footwear, food and water. They had no other alternative but to journey on foot towards their home state. In peak summer and hot tarred roads, they walked and walked for hundreds of miles with women and children; some did not live to reach the long awaited end. While most walked on highways, some walked on railway tracks. Many were killed by vehicles and goods trains as transportation of essential goods was allowed. Some died of sickness and dehydration.

Some were even raped and trafficked for sexual exploitation.

There's no account yet! There are no statistics. The government's attention was towards priorities. The migrants' journey was spotlighted by limited media coverage. The system did not bother about human rights despite criticism and outcry posted on social media.

There is still no official data on how many might have been driven to death by suicide in the traumatic months of the lockdown. But between March and July 2020, the news media alone reported 419 such deaths in the country. At a time when the Indian state should have shown its most benign, generous face, it ended up being intimidatory and draconian. And you did not have to travel to remote interior villages or to the hinterland to discover that food was running short. Any settlement of migrant workers, even just on the outskirts of the capital, would tell the same story – Barkha Dutt in her book 'To Hell and Back: humans of Covid'

The lockdown badly affected the general poor and the middle class families. Most people struggled with money needed for basic needs and medicines. Since medical and pharmaceutical related movements were allowed, first year student doctors and nurses were officially called to assist hospitals and Covid care facilities. This is what attracted the traffickers. They not only targeted the students, they lured other fresh enthusiastic girls to be paid interns!

Traffickers disguised themselves as online placement agents. Most idol youth had nothing better to do during the lockdown besides being online. Traffickers managed to make fake ID's and documents to transport the victims by road. They succeeded in pushing some ignorant girls into private flesh trade in some major cities like Bangalore far from their home towns. Some victims were sold to bride traffickers to become forced brides. Such incidences get leaked out to rescuers by paid informers before and after occurrence. Whenever the tip off was passed on in advance, in a few cases, victims were managed to get saved in North East India.

"Traffickers have also expanded their reach through the misuse of internet and communication technology to advertise, recruit and exploit persons, and especially lure children whom they groom for sexual online exploitation."The pandemic has impacted the capacity of governments and NGOs to provide essential services to victims."How can we continue to detect victims who are further hidden, or exploited from their own homes?"

https://www.reuters.com/article/us-global-trafficking-expertview-idUSKBN27300T

*An Imaginative Journey
of the Reality*

Select case history inputs from contributors

Part 1

*Disclaimer: All the following information in all parts is used
with permission. Names of all victims both minor and major*

have been changed to protect their identities. Co-incidence of names is not intentional and not subject to any disputes. There are no images submitted here. Some experiences revealed by victims are sensitive disclosers related to Child Sexual Abuse, Commercial Sexual Exploitation, Violence and Self Harm.

Prerana is a civil society organization that started working in the Red-Light Areas of Mumbai in 1986 first with a view to eliminate second generation trafficking (ESGT) i.e. trafficking of the children of trafficked victims into the sex trade, allied activities of sex trade or illegal labor. To achieve this Prerana evolved several path-breaking interventions, piloted them, built a success story out of each intervention, and disseminated them for wide mainstreaming. Prerana expanded the scope of its intervention to address the issues of the prostituted women of the RLAs specially to fight violence against them and to protect their legal and human rights. It also started addressing other child rights issues, gradually including working with children rescued from commercial sexual exploitation through Post Rescue Operations (PRO), children rescued from begging through its project 'Sanmaan' (the Honor), and child sexual maltreatment through its initiative 'Aarambh' (the Beginning). The work of Prerana has been recognized nationally and internationally as being at the forefront of leading the global fight against trafficking and sexual exploitation. Prerana means "inspiration" in Hindi and Sanskrit.

The following case stories in part one is a courtesy submission by Prerana

1A. Falling through the cracks in the system

Limitations in existing child care and protection services

During a routine visit to the CCI [child care institution], a social worker spotted a child sitting alone crying. The child, Zara, seemed visibly distressed and was incoherently speaking about how something was disturbing her. The social worker comforted her to calm down.

Sexual abuse and sexual exploitation - The child's narrative

The first interaction with Zara revealed that she had been sexually abused by her father in January 2018. She had mentioned this abuse to her mother earlier but it was overlooked. Her insensitive mother had warned Zara to maintain confidentiality and threatened her with dire consequences. The significant emotional distress caused by her father's act worsened after her mother's response. Feeling helpless, Zara ran away from home. A few days later, the police found Zara wandering on a beach. She told them about her trauma; the police took her for medical tests that resulted in pregnancy. Her pregnancy was terminated medically and she was shifted to a CCI.

The police registered a case of sexual abuse under the act of 'Protection of Children from Sexual Offences,' [POCSO]. Her father was subsequently arrested. In June 2018, Zara was restored to her family by an order passed by the Child Welfare Committee [CWC]. Zara's mother began to physically abuse her, blaming her for her father's arrest. She demanded Zara to withdraw her statement against her father. Experiencing a hostile environment at home, Zara ran away again.

September 2018, Zara was sleeping at a railway station where a young boy Salim befriended her with food. A few days later, Salim sold her to a woman called Mamta. Zara was raped by Mamta's husband. Mamta made a fake government ID of Zara, with her picture altered to depict that she was married by wearing a mangalsutra (traditional necklace worn by Hindu married girls) and a sindoor, (red colored mark on forehead) to pass her off as an adult. Zara was sexually abused by cheap customers for months before she was found by the police unconscious by the road in January 2019. She was medically stabilized and was presented before a different CWC closer to where she was found. This CWC was unaware of her history until Prerana's social worker talked to Zara there.

Indicators of psychological distress - The family's perspective

Prerana's social worker investigated Zara's mother. The mother said that Zara had run away from home with her brother when she was young. She added that Zara had attempted suicide when she was younger. The mother's disclosure indicated a hostile view of Zara. The mother's observations were that Zara had been affected mentally. Zara's maternal aunt said that often they had observed Zara talking to herself; she could not maintain her personal hygiene and would not bathe for days. They said that Zara had tried slitting her wrists in the past and had to be hospitalized too. It was observed that Zara's family was facing financial and health issues. They were not so literate and capable to understand and cope with Zara's abnormalities. They stigmatized her because she would react aggressively whenever they tried to help her. The mother wished Zara to be well, and was willing to cooperate with her rehabilitation but she was not prepared to accept her back. She believed that her husband had been falsely accused. An investigation report was submitted to the CWC, suggesting the need for psychiatric diagnosis and therapy for Zara.

Soon Zara was referred to a counselor. During the counseling sessions, Zara confided that she felt betrayed by her family, especially her parents. While her father sexually abused her, her mother had neglected her disregarding her symptoms. Despite these experiences, she ignorantly trusted her new friend Salim who deceived her! Recurring traumatic experiences left deep mental effects on Zara.

Mental Health in a Child Care Institution [CCI]

In the CCI, the social worker began regular interaction sessions with Zara. The social worker noted that Zara had difficulty in recalling past traumatic incidents and would get angry while talking about her family. Zara was so troubled by the past traumatic incidents that caused her nightmares of her father trying to harm her. These traumatic memories also affected Zara's interaction with others. The social worker observed that Zara was extremely fearful of men and feared to step out the CCI as she fearfully imagined her father waiting outside to harm her. The social worker observed that she would often repeat the narration of the past traumatic experiences.

During her visits to the CCI, the social worker would often get staff complaints of Zara's behavior. Zara expressed to the social worker that she felt mistreated by the fellow inmates and staff of the institution. She was stigmatized as a 'mentally unstable' and was mocked at by all of them. She would innocently ask why she was mocked at and ridiculed by the staffs who are supposed to be caretakers at CCI?

Such traumatic experiences affected Zara's perception and abilities to cope up. Zara began to perceive neutral comments and behaviors of others as threatening. During some interactions, the social worker observed that Zara would make violent threatening gestures towards other occupants if they would mock or criticize her. She would often find herself emotionally overwhelmed by such incidents and found it difficult to live with these negative experiences often resorting to self-harm or unusual crying patterns as a way of experiencing her distress.

Zara once confided to the social worker that she found physical pain much more manageable than the emotional pain she experienced. Hence, there were severe incidents of Zara hurting herself by eating brick powder, cutting herself with sharp objects and banging her head on the door. Her narratives also began to move towards thoughts of suicide. Zara would often share with the social worker that she did not feel worthy of living anymore. She was admitted to a psychiatric hospital for assistance, thrice a year. While she was hospitalized, Zara reported that she underwent Electro Convulsive Therapy (ECT) once and was subsequently put on medication. ECT is normally administered for 14 days to patients who are suicidal and who do not respond to medications. It was observed that the ECT and follow up medication stabilized Zara however it often caused her drowsiness and weakness. Psychiatric treatment is usually a long process for severe cases. Zara continued to be managed by medications with reduced dosage and psychosocial counseling.

1B. Story of Priya Mitra

Singing her way to a dignified life

Priya Mitra - a child from the notorious RLA (red light area) of Falkland Road in Mumbai. Until the age of 7, Priya was spotted loitering on the streets. This story traces her and her mother Neelam's journey from the well of darkness to a world where Priya now guards her rights, exercises choices and enjoys dignity. Her passion for singing has eventually opened up a new world for her.

In the scorching summer of 2012, the Prerana outreach team spotted the 7 year old scantily clad Priya loitering around unattended in the dusty lanes of Falkland Road. Children are particularly vulnerable in the RLA's of Mumbai, as pimps hunt for free and captive recruits in the vicinity. The outreach team found her mother Neelam, they discussed Priya's safety and the dangers of leaving her unattended in the streets.

Neelam was a victim of sex trafficking. She was trafficked in 2012, was held captive in a caged brothel. Brothel-keepers blocked movements by social workers in the area. Despite the challenges, Prerana's outreach team constantly made their way in when they had to. Neelam only knew Bengali language, she was informed about Prerana's Night Care Center (NCC) and services offered there for children. After some efforts and persuasion from another woman, Neelam enrolled her daughter Priya into the NCC.

It took over 3 months for Prerana's team to begin normal communication with Neelam. When she was convinced of her daughter's welfare, she felt comfortable with the team. She began confiding more about her past life and how she was trafficked. Language remained no more a barrier as Neelam learnt to interact in Hindi. Neelam originated from the eastern state of West Bengal. She had the responsibility of four children; three daughters and a son. Her husband was an alcoholic. Their financial situation worsened after his death. Her in-laws refused to support her. Neelam was left to fend for herself and her children. A village acquaintance offered to help her with a job in Mumbai. Forced by her circumstances, Neelam agreed. She was brought to Mumbai with one daughter. Neelam was sold to a brothel keeper. She was ignorant about what would happen to her in an unknown place. Her ordeal started when the brothel-keeper started torturing her to recover the money spent on buying her. She was routinely beaten up and starved. For the sake of her daughter, Neelam had to surrender. She never got any money from what she earned.

Neelam dreamt of good education for Priya in Mumbai, but her misery seemed endless. One of her customers promised to bring her out of the brothel. He promised to shift her to another place. He shifted her to another brothel where they lived together. Neelam managed to save some money but the man stole the money and fled. Neelam was disturbed and did not give up on her dreams of educating her daughter. "I will support her education as long as she wants to study. I will stay in Mumbai and give her the best education I can," she said.

At the mothers' meeting at Prerana, Neelam learnt many life skills like maintaining her accounts and finances, budgeting, saving and investing in insurance schemes. At such meetings Prerana discusses topics empowering the women. A year later, Neelam showed many improvements maintaining daily interactions with team Prerana.

Attempts were made to transfer Priya to a better school.

She was encouraged to attend study classes in the evening. Priya enthusiastically took part in activities such as little stars, puppet show, dancing, recreational and educational activities. She was interested in puppetry which was used as a medium to raise awareness on issues such as health, cleanliness, gender equality and behavior.

Priya learnt about child sexual abuse, unsafe and confusing touch, and personal safety. She also learnt about self-defense during the life skill activities. Gradually, Priya started to educate her friends about self-defense. She taught them the techniques to raise an alarm and how to strike back when attacked. At a young age, she displayed a sharp presence of mind. As Priya was 8 years old, she grew curious about activities in the red light area. She was curious to know why women stood by the roadside and why they painted (make-up) their faces.

Neelam felt the need to enroll Priya in the Day Care Center (DCC) facility. In 2013 Priya was enrolled in Prerana's DCC. Priya was enrolled into standard I at Khetwadi municipal school. Priya was a quick learner. She progressed as an active student, punctual in homework and was attentive. In 2014 Priya's teachers advised Prerana's to enroll her in the classes run by Indian Association for Promotion of Adoption & Child Welfare (IAPA), called Asmita classes. The classes were meant to supplement classroom teachings. Priya was taught to read, write and speak English apart from other activities. Recognizing her potential, IAPA offered her a monthly scholarship.

Parenting responsibilities aren't easy for mothers in the red-light areas. Here, for a mother her child is her family and vice-versa. Often, long absence of mothers, as happens in the sex trade, becomes an impediment in their active involvement in holistic development of their child. A child in the red-light area goes through a transient relationship and acceptance of one's mother doesn't come easy. This is where Prerana intervenes. Apart from the regular visits to a child's educational institutions, Prerana's Team also encourages mothers to get involved in the overall development of their children, a step in effective parenting.

In 2017, as Priya turned 11, she became a member of Ekta Group - the children's collective. Typically, children can join Ekta on completing 12 years of age. Priya's journey into singing started in 2013, when a voluntary organization 'Song Bound' approached Prerana to train the children in singing. Priya attended the sessions regularly.

In 2018, she became one of the eight children who were selected for the Yuva Arts Project, a cross culture event held in Canada.

Priya attends Prerana's morning study classes. "I enjoy English and science," said the 12 year old, always open to learning.

Every child deserves the right to education and a dignified life.

1C. Recognizing Potential Danger

A tale of three sisters

Children who go through traumatic experiences need special care and protection. A victimized child needs to be placed in a secure environment to begin the process of healing and rehabilitation. This process does not end at the placement of the child in a safe place, whether it is a children's home or repatriated family home. In cases where the child is placed in a children's home, it has been observed that the child often needs physical and mental health assistance at various stages.

While being appointed to provide assistance to a child, e.g. from a support person, caseworkers or social worker the aiding professionals might realize the need for further intervention. In some cases, the vulnerability of a child stems from their surroundings. In such cases, it raises the need to take preventive measures to ensure the safety of other children in the home

Here is one such case where Prerana had been appointed to medically assist a child. After interacting with the child, team Prerana realized the need to intervene more extensively. Over the course of the case, the team realized that this child was not the only one that needed help but her sisters were potential victims of commercial sexual exploitation too, who needed to be protected.

The child victim, Fauzia had been placed in a government rehabilitation home [CH] in 2016, after being rescued from commercial sexual exploitation. The JJ act mandates that the CWC hold an inquiry to undertake a social investigation to assess the personal, social and economic background of the child and its family. The

CWC is assisted by the social investigation report (SIR) to decide on the next course of action which also includes the decision on whether to restore the child to the family or a rehabilitation home.

The appointed organization had submitted the SIR which mentioned that Fauzia had two younger sisters. The mother had passed away and the father abandoned them. The sisters lived with their grandmother who had no steady source of income and was old and unfit. The SIR concluded that her home was not safe for Fauzia and she was vulnerable to be re-trafficked.

After being placed at the CH, Fauzia's condition manifested in abnormal behavior including self-harm. The CWC decided to admit the child to psychiatric treatment. In Feb 2017, team Prerana met with Fauzia and was appointed to assist the child at the hospital.

Upon interacting with Fauzia, it was discovered that no organization had been assigned to follow up with the child. Prerana wrote to the CWC requesting that the case be referred to them for follow up even though a social investigation had been completed. Team Prerana visited Fauzia's family to understand the case better.

The interaction with Fauzia revealed that she had an aunt whom she lived with. Upon meeting the aunt, the team learned that she was from the neighborhood and not biologically related. Bano, the aunt, was a neighbor who had rented out a room to Fauzia's grandmother and her sisters. Bano informed the Team that a maternal aunt of Fauzia lived nearby but refused the care of the girls.

Over the next few months, the team tried to convince Bano to get Fauzia's aunt to CWC but Bano did not cooperate. Subsequently, the team learned that Fauzia's grandmother passed away. They also learned that Fauzia's sister, Asma who had started to live with Razia, the biological aunt. In September 2017, the team paid a visit to Razia. The team observed that Razia was in her fifties. She did not share a good relationship with Fauzia because of her closeness with Bano. She alleged that Bano had pushed Fauzia into the sex trade along with Bano's own children. The team could not find any evidence to back this claim. The team also learned about the third sister Saba living with Bano.

The team followed up on Fauzia's case for months. The interactions with Fauzia revealed that Bano had earlier, allegedly attempted to sell off Fauzia to buyers at Hyderabad. She had also allegedly attempted to sell Saba. Fauzia also claimed that Bano sold narcotics. Despite all this, it was observed that Fauzia wanted to be restored to Bano! Fauzia did not have an alternative.

In January 2018, the team learned that Asma had moved out of Razia's home and was living with Bano again. Razia had informed the team about Bano's area as being unsafe and about Bano's alleged involvement in sex trade. The team felt that Asma and Saba's stay with Bano was a threat as both girls could be trafficked.

Based on a request from Prerana, summons was issued to the local police to present Asma and Saba before the CWC. Asma was brought but Saba could not be found. Asma spoke to the CWC about feeling unsafe with Razia as Razia's daughter's boyfriend had molested her. Asma had complained to Razia who did not believe her, so Asma moved to Bano's home.

Since the child did not speak of exploitation by Bano and was keen on living with her, the CWC decided against admitting her in a children's home. Meanwhile, the team followed up to check on Fauzia who had been transferred to a different CH. The CWC also asked Asma to visit her sister at the CH every month.

In May 2018, the team got a call from Razia, informing them that Asma had been placed in a CH. The team inquired on how Asma had been admitted to the CH and found out that Asma was caught in a fight between Bano's son and a neighbor. The neighbor had torn Asma's clothes in the scuffle. Bano had taken Asma to the police station to lodge an FIR. Since a minor had been sexually harassed, it opened up as a case of sexual abuse for action by the CWC.

Prerana requested to be appointed as a support organization in Asma's case as they had done investigations of the family which would help to rehabilitate Asma. Team Prerana had challenges of finding a vacancy in CH. Asma was transferred to a different CH. Following routine medical tests at that CH, it was detected that she was HIV positive. After initial interactions with the superintendent the transmission of the virus was unknown. Asma has made no disclosure about sexual abuse, though that possibility could not be ruled out at that stage.

Asma has shown considerable improvement at the CH. The team has been regularly following up on both girls. Asma was interested in education, but since she had never been to school it was not possible to get her enrolled in a school. The team is currently working on alternative ways for her to pursue education. Meanwhile, she has been taking vocational training. As a result of counseling sessions, her mental health had improved. The team observed positive results. From an initially reserved child, she became more expressive and in control of her emotions. She engages with everybody and participates in the various activities that are held at the

CH. Her physical health improved with proper diet and HIV medications.

Fauzia completed 18 years of age and has been transferred to an aftercare facility in Mumbai suburbs. It was a challenge for the team to convince her not to go back to Bano. The third sister, Saba has also been through a series of traumatic experiences. The lack of a support system had made her dependent on alcohol. The team had made a number of visits to locate the missing Saba.

1D. Fighting for a Future

A story of rescue and rehabilitation

The prostituted women living in RLAs have little to no agency. Often they are under close control of their brothel keeper or aadmi (male pimp), with little voice of their own. Here is one such case of a prostituted mother who was forced to leave her child in the hands of her brothel keeper, but continued to fight the odds to rescue her child.

At the age of 16, Champa was trafficked into the RLA of Kamathipura in Mumbai from her village in West Bengal by a man belonging to her village. She continued to live in Kamathipura for four years, after which she returned to her village and stayed there for a few months. She was forced to leave her village due to constant fights as her family and neighbors from her village were aware that she was in the sex trade and lived in Kamathipura. She moved to Pune's Budhwar Peth RLA as she had heard about the same during her time in Kamathipura.

Champa lived in a brothel there. A regular customer got friendly with her, from whom she got impregnated. On finding that out Champa's brothel keeper got furious and went to the extent of getting rid of that particular customer. Two months into her pregnancy, around July 2015, the Andhra Pradesh Police conducted a raid in the Budhwar Peth RLA to take action against the brothel keepers and rescue the victims. Instead of the brothel keeper, the police arrested Champa and put her in prison. She was in prison for one month after which the brothel keeper bailed her out and claimed to have spent 350 thousand as her bail amount. To avoid regularly presenting Champa at the court, the brothel keeper sent her away to Delhi. She returned to Pune's Budhawar Peth to give birth to her daughter Sanya who was born in January 2016 in Pune. Champa was able to repay 100 000 rupees to the brothel keeper and was attempting to pay off the rest. The brothel keeper would physically assault Priya and would keep Sanya away from her for a long time. She couldn't tolerate any longer and left Budhawar Peth. She moved to Kamathipura in 2017. The brothel keeper at Budhawar Peth had kept baby Sanya in her custody, stating that she would return her after Champa paid up the loan.

Upon returning to Kamathipura, Champa came in contact with some Civil Society Organizations (CSO) working in the RLA. She narrated her ordeal to the CSOs hoping that one of them would help reunite her with Sanya. Champa then met the team of Mumbai Smiles, an organization that works with the underprivileged communities in Mumbai. Mumbai Smiles has been collaborating with Prerana since August 2017 and has been running a play school at Prerana's Falkland road center.

Mumbai Smiles had not worked on such cases earlier, they approached the Prerana outreach team and shared Champa's concerns. The team met Champa during an outreach visit where she disclosed that the brothel keeper had kept Sanya's original birth certificate and Champa's Pan Card and was not willing to return it. A Mumbai Smiles representative also informed the team that they had interacted with a woman named Pooja who was taking care of Sanya at Budhwar Peth. Pooja was taking care of three other children of the women living in the brothel.

The team informed Champa that they would need to approach the Child Welfare Committee (CWC) regarding the case. They helped her understand the role of the CWC and details of the process that would be followed. Champa was also instructed that she would have to mention her experience to the CWC and to the police officials.

On 6th December 2018, the social workers of Prerana approached Mumbai's CWC informing them about this case. They reiterated that a rescue needed to be conducted as the victim was in need of special care. The social workers from Prerana continued to meet with Champa to discuss procedures that had to be followed before and after the rescue. Champa agreed to direct the team to the brothel from a distance to avoid being identified. The CWC passed an order to the Social Service Branch (SSB) of Pune Police to locate, rescue and present the child.

Around 2:30 pm the social workers and the SSB team went into the Budhwar Peth RLA to conduct the rescue. The brothel keeper fled. The team found out that Champa had leaked out information of the rescue to Pooja the babysitter.
The rescue team searched the brothel, they couldn't find the child. The rescue team went to the babysitter's house. The house was locked, Pooja had moved. The rescue team returned to the brothel and picked up two women for questioning. The social workers tried calling Pooja, she finally answered and told them that a man would be visiting the police station to talk to them. He claimed to be working with an organization that works with HIV positive women. He supported the brothel keeper and Pooja saying that they were taking care of Sanya because Champa abandoned her. After much argument, he agreed to call Pooja to get Sanya to the police station. Pooja brought her. The police kept her at a temporary child shelter.

12th December, the case was presented to the CWC. The CWC ordered the restoration of the child to her mother. The order also stated that Sanya would avail Prerana's Night Care services and spend time with her mother during the day.

At Prerana's NCC, while looking after Sanya, the NCC staff noticed she hadn't attained key developmental growth compared to all three year olds. She would not speak and had to be toilet trained. She was taken to hospital for speech therapy. The therapist diagnosed that until she could process what she heard, she wouldn't be able to form a reply. The therapist suggested an ENT specialist.

A few months later, as Champa would skip regular meetings, this affected the child. Sanya was unable to recognize Champa as her mother and wouldn't readily go to her, Champa in her anxiety would try to be harsh with Sanya to get her to respond with love towards her.

Champa was asked to spend more time with her child to help recognize and identify her as a mother. They would also encourage Sanya to call Champa 'mumma' and help her understand that Champa was her mother.

In June 2019, Champa spoke to the Prerana team stating her inability to care for Sanya after the NCC hours. She expressed her desire to enroll Sanya into a CCI. The Team discussed procedures to which Champa agreed. Sanya was enrolled into Asha Sadan, a CCI in the city.

Champa continues to live in a brothel in Kamathipura's 11th lane. She regularly visits Sanya at Asha Sadan. Sanya is adjusting well to her new environment. She has also been growing closer to her mother.

An Imaginative Journey of the Reality

Part 2

Transforming Lives Foundation

The following inputs are from Transforming Lives Foundation [TLF] based in the western suburbs of Mumbai with whom I worked and volunteered for certain periods since 2011. Some of the stories below have my involvement. Names of all victims and accused have been changed to avoid complications.

TLF is a Christian Ministry which used to be called Operation Rahab and was founded by Manohar Waghela in 2010. TLF's mission purpose is assisting the Indian criminal justice system in co-ordination with the police to prevent crimes related to Sex Trafficking. TLF focuses on rescues' of minor girls and majors forced into prostitution. Until 2021 TLF has conducted more than 100 successful rescue operations, rescued 482 survivors of which 110 girls were minors. 400 survivors have been successfully rehabilitated back into mainstream society. 30 of TLF's survivors are employed and 12 of them are completing their education.

Despite funding challenges due to the ban on FCRA license, TLF continues with specific rescues till date.

2A. Sweet talker Brother in Law

Bhavesh was originally from Ahmadabad, capital of the state of Gujarat in western India. He was married to a Gujarati homemaker and lived with her in Mumbai. He earlier had a job as a salesman of products meant for beauty parlors and ladies hair salons. A few years passed by, he settled in the market and maintained public relations with mostly women entrepreneurs and managers. He learnt about the dirty business attached to some parlors in the suburbs. In that period shady massage parlors were booming and were mostly owned by small-time politicians. Soon, Bhavesh gave up his job and began his independent business of beauty products. At least four times a year he would travel to Ahmadabad which is about seven hours away by train, to visit his folks sometimes with his wife and sometimes alone. He would carry along beauty products to give away as gifts to his 22 year old sister in law [wife's sister] Bhavna. She was an educated, young, innocent, attractive and a career aspirant girl. His wife Rajni was unaware of the friendship that had developed between Bhavesh and Bhavna. Secretly Bhavna was lured to meet Bhavesh at the train station one day. He promised her opportunities in the beauty products company. She told her folks that she was going for an interview in Mumbai.

In Jan 2010, as they arrived in Borivali, they stayed at a small hotel. There he entertained her with alcohol and food and raped her for three days. He photographed and video-graphed her nudity and shared the posts with potential clients on social media. She was impregnated. That was the cause for her to be rejected by most clients. She was finally sold to a massage parlor owner at Mira road.

One evening of July 2011, I was on surveillance duty outside a line of massage parlors in Mira road. Those days massage parlors would lure customers for commercial sexual acts in their back rooms. While I pretended to lean on the bus stop railing and speak on the mobile, facing a parlor, I saw Bhavna standing outside the entrance wiping her flowing tears. I reported to my boss at the NGO and was advised to engage her. I stepped in and told Bhavna that I just need my shoulders to be massaged. She asked for the payment, I paid with a 50% tip. As she stood behind me and massaged my shoulders, she whispered me "you are the first customer I met to tip me half of the full payment." I smiled and replied softly, "because I think you needed it." As I watched her facial expressions interacting with me in the mirror, I recorded her through the mirror. She seemed melancholic as she asked me with an emotional voice "why I was so kind amongst everybody else who were rude and abusive?" I replied "I try my best to be kind to people, I felt sorry to see you crying outside, I did not actually intend to get a massage, but, I stepped in to talk to you." I asked her what was wrong with her. With a finger on her lips, she responded by whispering in my ear, that she would explain later as her boss was with a client next door. She asked for my number, which I immediately gave. My encounter with her was fully captured on my spy camera. I left before her boss could come out; she gave me a big smile, shook my hand, then she made a sign gesture that she would call me.

I got a call from her at 4 AM the next morning. She apologized for waking me up. She said that I was a unique customer who just asked for a shoulder massage and paid the whole amount for the complete package. I realized her need for my friendship on the phone, she cried and told me her story briefly and she asked me if I could help get her out of captivity and go back home with her baby girl. I responded that she could hope and trust me to fulfill her desire. Bhavna's baby girl was kept by the owner as a token of blackmail and enslavement. I noted down her owner's name and number.

As the few hours of dawn passed, Bhavna's case was reported to my boss and to Atul Aher, then Assistant Inspector of Police, AHTU [Anti Human Trafficking Unit] Mira Bhayandar area. We soon held a meeting and set up a plan to send our team member as a decoy customer to the owner of the massage parlor. The decoy customer visited the owner and said that he was very satisfied with her service; he tipped her and said that he would return again with his friend. The encounter was recorded. He requested another comfortable place for a longer encounter as the parlor was too compact. She invited him to her apartment which was at another location. This place was out of the jurisdiction of the AHTU police. The visit to the apartment happened the next day. The baby girl was spotted and recorded at the apartment before she was taken away by the maid.

The trap for the raid was preset with after the case was reported to the Deputy Commissioner of Police [DCP] of that particular zone. As the decoy team left the apartment, the owner was picked up and taken to the police station. At the same time Bhavna was rescued by me and the AHTU police team. Her statement and FIR [first information report] against Bhavesh was filed, she was kept at a temporary shelter home and was content with my plans and actions to help her. Bhavesh was arrested and charged by the AHTU police.

The owner of the parlor had influential links with small-time corrupt politicians who had been bribing the corrupt police staff of that station. The police tried their best to avoid the owner's arrest and to avoid rescuing the baby. They manipulated the case with lies and managed to change the story to the DCP.

Manohar argued the case at the police station and spoke to the DCP again asking him to speak to the AHTU inspector who told him that we have recorded evidence of the victim, the owner and the baby. Bhavna was taken by Atul Aher's team to the Kandivili police station and the copy of her statement to AHTU and FIR was submitted. Within 15 minutes the baby girl was brought to the police station and handed over to the Bhavna with a written apology.

The case crashed without charges on the parlor owner due to the manipulation of the corrupt police staff. Bhavna later testified in court. Bhavesh's bail was rejected. Months later, he was convicted by the Thane district court of rape and trafficking as AHTU submitted a strong charge sheet against him. He was sentenced to 14 years imprisonment. His wife Rajni filed for an automatic divorce which was granted by the family court.

Bhavna's dad came to escort his daughter back from the shelter home. I was called to visit the AHTU station while they would be there. Rajni was there too. Bhavna joined the palms of her hands and broke into tears of joy as she saw me walk into the entrance of the AHTU station. They others clapped in applause. She cried with tears dripping on my shirt as she hugged me, she then bowed down and touched my feet [expression of high respect in Hindu tradition.] As a lady police constable held the peacefully calm baby Shristi, Bhavna's father completed the same gesture of touching my feet as he verbally thanked me with his joined palms. Rajni joined her hands to express gratitude too and she stood next to Bhavna... both of them wiping their dripping tears.

Standing next to Atul Aher, I was too overwhelmed with a double portion of joy...their joy plus my joy! I was emotionally choked to say anything but responded most of the time by smiling. The AHTU team were also thanked by Bhavna's family with joined palms.

The next day, Bhavna and her family left for Ahmadabad. She called me to say bye from the railway station. She called again after she reached home and expressed her gratitude again saying "God sent you in my life," "yes, that's true," I responded. I advised her to change her number; remain disconnected from social media and find a decent job. She followed my advice and settled down peacefully with her parents. She still sends me greetings on festive occasions and my birthday. She has a good job, lives with Rajni and her baby who is now [at the time of this writing] a bright little school girl. Bhavna wants to motivate her child to be a senior police officer. This case is hard to forget for me as much as it is for Bhavna and her family.

Although we were disappointed with the acquittal of the parlor owner, we were heart fully glad about Bhavna and her restoration. We were satisfied with the conviction of Bhavesh. Thanks to inspector Atul Aher for his integrity and the AHTU police team of Mira Bhayandar area.

2B. Another Parlor Story

Massage parlors were a thriving business for commercial sex in the suburbs off Mumbai between the years 2010 and 2012.

In December 2011, based on a tip off received I was asked to go and visit a particular massage parlor at Bhayandar west to find an alleged minor girl there. I went there and spotted a short girl with a small physical frame. She seemed to be under 18 years old but she wasn't. I asked if I could be serviced by her. I was told to wait for a while. As I waited in the waiting room, seated next to me at a distance of about 3 feet was a man in colored apparel who seemed to be a cop. He was busy involved in a cheerful conversation with two other girls in their local language. I got him and the girls captured in about 10 minutes of recording before I went in. As she began massaging my forehead and shoulders, I recorded her and then pretended to check my messages. Soon I told her that I got an urgent message and I had to leave. She got her payment and I left.

I submitted the recording at our NGO office and it was soon reported to the AHTU Mira Bhayandar police. Inspector Atul Aher reported the case to his senior officer the Deputy Superintendent of Police [DySP] Thane district. They investigated and found out that the man joking with the girls at the parlor was a cop off duty attached to Bhayandar police station. A complete report of illegal massage parlors operational in Bhayandar west was submitted to the DySP. The next day the DySP set up a meeting with the municipal commissioner and AHTU police. They organized a raid to uproot all illegal parlors in Bhayandar west. With all resources of manpower, vehicles and equipment they headed for Bhayandar west.

Within two days of my reporting, the police completed a massive sweep of 18 massage parlors. Girls were rescued, managers and owners were arrested, customers were reprimanded with fines and warnings, and structures of all 18 parlors were demolished by municipal bulldozers.

None of the rescued girls were minor; most of them were working as per their own will. Just 2 of them among 88 were forced victims. The rest were let off with warnings and written apologies. The accused were charged and later convicted. The corrupt cop of Bhayandar police station was terminated from service post investigations. The AHTU and Thane police managed to conduct this raid without our involvement. Later the DySP called us for facilitation and handed over a certificate of appreciation for effective reporting.

2C. Trapping the Mechanical Engineer

In March 2020 the first Covid 19 pandemic call for a nationwide lockdown in India was abruptly declared by the government with just a few hours of notice. This affected businesses, transportation, jobs, institutions and families....almost everyone were caught in the unpreparedness and panic just as the government was.

Besides daily wage workers suddenly affected by poverty, the lower middle class salaried people who usually find it difficult to save from limited 'hand to mouth' earnings were equally affected as they had bills, installments and fees as dues to pay. The unemployed educated youth were frantically looking for freelance opportunities to work online, while some would be ready to do any kind of work like loading and unloading essential goods to survive. Boys were involved in selling fruits, vegetables, fish or such essentials on the street at limited allowed time periods. Girls couldn't do much as the boys did, so they were more desperately looking for sources of income online.

Neha was an educated degree holder girl in her early twenties desperately looking for work online. She posted her free ad on the OLX app. She did something she was not supposed to do - she shared her contact number and address.

Viswakarma was a young qualified jobless mechanical engineer with a crooked mindset looking for such vulnerable prey on the internet. He had some past experience of lurking and selling girls to traffickers. He was excited about girls looking for jobs via postings on social media. He called Neha, spoke to her in English and befriended her with sweet talk promising a good company job with a salary of 30000 rupees. A few months later, the lockdown was relaxed with limitations. Restaurants were allowed to be open for limited times following social distancing procedures. Neha was called to a restaurant for a treat. Viswakarma took a few of her photographs saying that he would use it to increase the chances of getting her a job. Vishvakarma morphed Neha's images with nude images and started blackmailing her to satisfy his customers. Neha fearfully submitted to his pressurized demands and she was used by customers arranged by Vishvakarma. Customers were charged rupees 8000 from which she got 2000.

This is how her story got exposed

In December 2020 as the first lockdown was coming to a 75% relaxation, Manohar started using the 'Tinker' dating App to find girls posting ads. He found Shobha, a 19 year old who had mentioned her number. He began communicating with her and since she was a professional, she offered her services boldly. Manohar lured her and asked for another girl besides her. She sent images and details of four other girls including Neha. Manohar then figured out that she could be a trafficker or a pimp working under a bigger criminal.

A few hours later, a deal was made for five girls to visit five men for a full day sex party at a private bungalow. The AHTU Mira Bhayandar police were alerted and they led the case with the Vasai police. The location was set at Vasai, a north western busy suburban town about 50 KM from south Mumbai. The amount of rupees 15000 per girl was agreed upon and an advance payment was done by Manohar with marked currency. He received the five attractive girls at the Vasai railway station and offered them cold beverages at the stall so that we could spot Vishvakarma watching the girls.

As Manohar was introduced to the four other girls who spoke in English, he was shocked to know that one of them had completed Masters in Arts!, the second (Neha) was a graduate in commerce, the third was in the 12th grade and the fourth was a graduated employee with a renowned automobile company – Mahindra and Mahindra Ltd. They all were in the age group of 18 and 26.

Vishvakarma, the criminal boss of the girls, was at the station platform nearby watching the girls. Eye contact between him and Shobha was noted by us. He did not interact with Manohar. But, as he was predicted to be there, he was being watched by me and 3 undercover AHTU police women split into 2 teams. One undercover lady cop pretended to hold me as a partner as we moved closer to his position. Vishvakarma's facial and eye movements were secretly being recorded. As Manohar led the girls to his car, Vishvakarma quickly followed in an auto rickshaw. He was followed by us on motor bikes. Soon as the girls reached the bungalow, Shobha paused to check her messages and make eye contact with Vishvakarma. He did not notice the surveillance team as we stepped in a nearby restaurant from where we could watch him. We reported his movements and appearance to the AHTU raid team leader inside and requested the police dogs to be brought with their handlers from the rear side of the bungalow closer to the western front. None of the police team members were in uniform or in police vehicles so they could hide their identity.

Once inside the bungalow, the girls' mobiles were confiscated, their bags were checked for drugs or weapons, the marked currency was taken, and Shobha revealed that her boss was waiting outside the bungalow. Vishvakarma was spotted by approaching cops; he tried to run as the area was open closer to the beach. He was soon chased and pulled down by the unleashed black Doberman named Blackbelt! The other German Shepherd Challenger ran around to trap the criminal from the front. He was bitten in two places, and was terrified with the bleeding bites caused by the jaw hold of both dogs.

He was soon charged with multiple offenses that could get him a life sentence! The 19 year old Shobha was charged with ITPA [prevention of immoral trafficking act] which rewards a minimum of seven years in prison! A young life misled into a ruined future. They are both under trials at the time of this writing as the case is subjudice.

The rest of the girls were sent to a shelter home for counseling sessions that lasted a hard three months. Their families were informed and counseled as well before they could be reinstated.

2D. A Rich Woman Trafficker

In India bribes are offered to corrupt higher officials or politicians to get business approvals or licenses issued faster, bribes sometimes are in the form of material gifts like vehicles, bribes are also known to be in the form of gifted sexual pleasure. Private apartments are rented or rooms in high end hotels are booked for such services rendered to them with attractive young girls.

This is a recent story dated December 2021. The lady accused is charged but still under trial. Her bail is refused.

Jayshriben is a real estate builder's wife; a rich woman, from Rajkot in the state of Gujarat living at a luxurious sea facing bungalow in Nalla Sopara about 55 KM from south Mumbai. She did not have her own children hence she did not know the value of children. She had ample time in her hands as she had servants to do her errands while her husband was busy spending 12 hours a day at work.

She had a favorite hobby to make money; she enjoyed luring local girls by showing them impressive luxury at her house, trips to the mall and treats in restaurants. She befriended them, gave them gifts, and began entertaining them with pornographic videos as their friendship advanced with mental and emotional conditioning. They were young ignorant girls from good families. Gradually she taught them to earn from pleasure and would escort them to hotel rooms and private apartments for encounters with rich clients in exchange of big amounts of cash. She would give the girl a big amount for the first time and smaller amounts subsequently. She wouldn't threaten, physically abuse or blackmail them. She brain washed them with kindness, pleasure, fun and money and used them during daytimes.

Her crooked husband booked the girls to please some of his clients.

Her information was leaked out to Manohar by a paid informer. Manohar started speaking to her on the phone in her language pretending to be a big time businessman. He named a local politician from whom he got her number. She believed Manohar. She offered girls even before Manohar could ask! Manohar did not show haste but showed interest in inviting girls for an upcoming business mens' weekend party. She sent him images of five attractive girls in seductive apparel out of whom two seemed to be minors. She said that three of them were readily available at her apartment while the two others were not ready at that time. Manohar did not want to waste time to rescue minors and accepted her invitation to visit her private apartment.

Manohar passed on the information to senior officers who instructed the Vasai police to raid the apartment. The raid was conducted, Jayshriben was picked up, three girls were rescued, and two of them were minors. The major victim was just 19. Two of them were students while the 19 year old was employed. The two students were promised good jobs. In their statements they disclosed they were lured two months ago and had served five to nine clients each.

At the police station her husband, with much confidence, came to bail her out. The only possibility was if Manohar withdrew his police complaint. He tried to convince Manohar who refused and threatened him that he could be implicated in a fresh complaint. The next day Manohar got a few calls from small time politicians to withdraw the case. One of them said that the builder was offering him a bribe of 800,000 rupees. Manohar refused, the court refused bail. And Jayshriben is now awaiting conviction.

The two minors were sent to CCI and the teen was sent to a shelter home. The court will decide on further steps to be taken for the victims.

2E. Promiscuous Mother Trafficker

Many bars unlike the strip clubs of the US, in Mumbai with call girls dancing to local hits had rooms at the back or in the basement to tempt drunken customers to be ripped off! The girls weren't forced victims. The state government banned such bars in 2005. Some of them were still functioning to fill pockets of corrupt officials.

In June 2015 I got a call from an informer. He told me

about a young slut bar dancer wanting to sell her virgin younger sister. I informed my boss Manohar and went to that bar undercover along with my colleague. I just had the name of that girl. We were well dressed, were wearing fake jewelry and smelled aromatic, carrying hidden cameras. We found her and visually expressed our desire for her; we asked her to sit for a while and offered her a drink of beer with us. I praised her beauty and asked her if she had sisters as sexy as she! When she smilingly asked why? I replied "for enjoyment at a private house party." She then said that she had to go as it was her turn to dance again and with a flirty gesture she bent before my face, making eye contact with her flirty eyes, she smilingly whispered that she would be back. She must have wrongly calculated that she turned me on!

After she returned, as I stared smilingly at her, my partner clapped and said wow; we praised her for her dancing and ordered another beer for her. Then she asked me how many boys would be at the party. I replied, just the two of us. "That's all"? She asked smilingly. Yes, I replied smilingly, it would be an all night party. Then she asked, how many girls we would need. My partner replied two or three. She said that her charges would be 15 K and her sister's charge would be more! I asked what was so special about her sister. She replied "she is a virgin, and whoever desires to break her virginity should pay up the extra amount in advance to my mother!" "Oh… how much"? I asked, she said "speak to her mother.' I agreed. My partner asked her for the address and contact numbers. She shared 2 numbers and saved our numbers too. She said to call the next day for the address. We agreed and pretended to be very excited. Then she said she had to go again, so we settled the bill with a good tip and left.

She was Shakshi, the bold and beautiful who seemed to be 25 years old. They lived in a two bedroom ownership apartment in a lower middle class area of Mira road. As soon as we entered the apartment, we were greeted and seated. Shakshi was so glad about the opportunity and offered us soft drinks. She then introduced us to her good looking tall and slim mother Radhika, she was scantily dressed and seemed to be 35-36! I guessed the mother to be a prostitute too. As they spoke to each other in their Marwari dialect, I asked if they were from Rajasthan. Her mom replied "yes", and asked me "where would be the private party"? I replied "at my residence" - I named a high status building close by in Mira road. She asked if I owned the apartment, I replied yes. Then she asked about my family. I said that I was divorced and had no kids…my parents had traveled abroad to the US. I asked her "how come she looked so young as a mother of Shakshi?" She felt flattered and replied that Shakshi was not her real daughter, but she was her husband's first wife's daughter and her mother had abandoned her in childhood. Soon later she turned towards the bedroom to call out her virgin daughter Simran. The greed of money blended with the innocence of Simran in the air as Radhika smilingly completed the act of introduction with the hope of achievement in her thoughts.

Simran was a tender looking medium framed school girl of 14 years to my perception of rescuing her from the clutches of a trafficker's evil intention. Her mother boldly said she would join Shakshi at the party. Without any expression of shock, I smiled and agreed. She said that we would have to pay 30000 for her and 15000 for Shakshi the day when we would come to pick them up. I agreed. But I asked the mother if Simran would cooperate. She replied, "yes, she knows what she has to do! Ask her," she told me! So, I asked Simran ``do you know that you would have to drink, dance and sleep with us." She innocently and smilingly replied with a programmed answer - "yes!"

It was a Thursday, as we prepared to leave them; we were asked "when would be the party?" My partner replied with excitement "this Saturday, we will come at 5 PM to pick them up with the cash payment." They exchanged full smiles and showed off their erotic apparel as we said "good bye, see you on Saturday."

During our visit, my partner Rohinton did not speak much and was busy recording the whole episode. The verification was reported to Manohar who reported to Inspector Atul Aher of AHTU police.

On Saturday we were prepared with bundles of 45000 rupees of marked currency. We called them to break the good news. As discussed, we went up to the apartment to pick up the girls at 5 PM. They were well dressed for a party. We handed over the marked currency and within 5 minutes Manohar and the raid team with 6 WPC's [women police constables] entered to arrest them, while we walked out. They panicked. Radhika started tearing the scanty clothes she was wearing and Shakshi pretended to faint. Simran was blank with the mouth open in shock.

They were taken to the AHTU station and questioned. Simran's statement was registered and she was sent for medical tests and then admitted to the CCI as ordered by the CWC. Radhika was the main accused and charged with ITPA and Shakshi was charged with harboring the accused. On the next day, Radhika's husband brought a lawyer with a bail application which was rejected. Shakshi's biological mother called me from Jaipur to offer an apology and said that she was unaware of her daughter's doings. She told me that Radhika was a promiscuous woman. She begged me to withdraw the case against Shakshi. I replied saying nothing could be done.

Five months later, Radhika was sentenced to seven years. Shakshi was sentenced to three years of corrective imprisonment which included rehabilitation and sessions to adapt to new productive skills.

2F. Howrah Bombay Mail

The historical city of Calcutta [now Kolkata] is about 300 years old. It was the capital city for the East India Company during the early years of British rule in India. It is the most populated city in India that connects interstate routes to the entire North Eastern part of India and Bangladesh. Sonagachi in Kolkata is known to be the largest RLA in Asia with multi-storey brothels accommodating about 50,000 commercial sex workers. Besides Sonagachi the other RLAs of Kolkata are in Bow Bazaar and Matiya areas.

Howrah is the main station in Kolkata for interstate and intercity mail and express trains. It has been commonly used by traffickers to board trains destined to Delhi or Mumbai. In the past two decades Police and NGOs teams have increased surveillance to trap traffickers and release victims there.

A NGO partnership effort by the surveillance team there called Manohar to inform about two girls being transported to Mumbai by a group of eight boys by Howrah Bombay Mail. All their photographs were sent while this group was in the 30 hours journey. Manohar split up the teams into three to wait at stations in Mumbai where there were possibilities for them to get off the train. They got off at the last terminating station CST. At CST they split into two. A group of seven boys split and went towards a busy commercial area called Kalbadevi. They were followed and their residence was noted. The other boy along with 2 girls went by a local train to Turbhe, an industrial area with a RLA of approximately 80 brothel shacks closely connected. Outside Turbhe station, they boarded an auto rickshaw that was waiting for them. The rickshaw went towards the RLA. Two team members boarded another rickshaw. There was a police check point that did not stop the suspected rick, but stopped the followers to question the two boys. The boys were trained not to disclose the truth to police as the police has corrupt elements within its system that leaks out information. Since the police were not satisfied with answers from the boys, they kept them in custody all night.

The next day Manohar approached the DCP in South Mumbai to request help to track down the seven boys living at Kalbadevi. The DCP suggested finding the girl first or the questioning of the seven boys may cause the alleged trafficker to flee. Manohar agreed and set up two teams to do 24 hours surveillance at Turbhe RLA to find the girls. Since the RLA area sewage system was under repairs, portable toilets were placed for the residents there. One of the two girls was spotted using the portable toilet. She was tracked and the house brothel was identified. The next day a fake customer from the NGO was sent to visit that house. He engaged that particular girl who did not reveal much information. The matter was shared with the south DCP who referred them to the DCP in charge of Turbhe area. The DCP at Turbhe asked them to go to the local police station. The local police station heard the case and leaked out information of the possibility of a raid. The complete Turbhe RLA remained shut making it impossible for the NGO team to proceed. Manohar went back to the DCP and informed him what happened. The DCP then set up his own team and conducted the raid in coordination with Manohar's team. Both the girls were picked up, including the alleged transporter and the brothel owner. Among the two girls, one of them was the transporter's documented wife. The other girl was the victim, battered and bruised with visible scars of torture. It was four days since her arrival and she had not yet agreed to sell her body. She was tortured and raped by two acquaintances there. The seven boys at Kalbadevi were picked up by police and questioned. They happened to be co-travelers who were befriended by Iqbal the trafficker to avoid suspicion at Howrah station.

In November 2008, the 17 year old victim Noori was medically treated, counseled, moved to a CCI and reinstated back to her family in WB.

Eight months later the court convicted her rapists Narendra and Ainuddin to rigorous imprisonment [RI] of 6 years each. Sonia the brothel keeper was sentenced to 7 years. Bijoy the trafficker got a ten years sentence and his wife Shahida got 5 years imprisonment.

2G. Rohit the gay Trafficker

This story is dated 2010, when images and videos could not be sent on phone messenger apps.

Rohit was a 35 year old gay known as Rohit Mehendiwala [mehendi artist]. Mehendi is a leaf green paste made by crushing Henna plant leaves. It is used to paint designs on hands, forearms and feet of girls or women in India. Such designs are like temporary tattoos and are usually done by women just before an occasion.

Rohit was a street artist seated outside the Maxus mall at Bhayandar in North Mumbai. Besides mehendi designing, he would also offer young girls to learn the art of mehendi at no costs! Since he was a gay, young girls would not shy from him. Income earned from being a street artist is meager. Rohit was a rich man because he earned by supplying girls to private customers at their homes or at lodges. He would influence young girls with dreams of jobs in modeling and the movie industry by showing them morphed photographers of him and movie stars.

Mansi and her neighbor friend Vandana were two innocent school going Marathi speaking girls belonging to lower middle class families living within walking distance from the mall. Like most girls, they were fond of mehendi art. They desired to learn the art from Rohit. Mansi was an orphan, her grandfather was looking after her. Vandana's parents spoke to Mansi's grandfather and allowed both of them to learn from Rohit since it was summer vacation time for schools.

A lodge worker spotted Rohit outside the mall from the food court outlet on the ground floor of the mall.

His close friend worked as a waiter in that outlet and watched Rohit regularly. The lodge worker told his friend that Rohit would sometimes bring young girls to the lodge. The waiter, who knew Manohar, passed on this information to him.

Rohinton posed as rich customer reached that lodge. He set up a call to Rohit through the worker there. Rohit came with photographs of girls and talked to Rohinton. He was asked to bring the two virgin girls Mansi and Vandana the next morning and was paid an advance of 1000 rupees. The deal was set for 20000 rupees.

Next morning the raid and rescue to trap Rohit was set up in co-ordination with DySP Thane District police standing by in the nearby street. Morning time was set, so that the court could be approached the same day.

Rohit Mehendiwala gets the two lured innocent girls in an auto rickshaw. Manohar and Rohinton were in the lodge. A team member watching the entrance of the lodge signaled the cops. The gay criminal yelled in panic with his palms on his cheeks as soon as he saw the cops, the girls were comfortably taken aside by WPCs and given beverages. Rohit got his pretty face reddish as he was tightly slapped by four WPCs! He was handcuffed and made to sit on the floor before being taken for a joy ride!

Mansi and Vandana were just 13 year olds, they were unharmed, and as ordered by the court they were handed over the same day to their families.

Rohit engaged an expensive defense lawyer, who bailed him out after 20 days of judicial custody. The trial went on for a long period as loopholes of lack of evidence and 'no harm done' to the victims were noted. In June 2011, I was sent to get details of the case from the Thane police DySP office. The DySP told me that even if Rohit is acquitted, he would not repeat the same crime again as he was given a very hard time under judicial custody. The cops alerted this case to all state and interstate police authorities This case was subjudice in 2012.

Later we did not bother to get information about what was the trial court's judgment. Our motive to rescue the innocent girls unharmed was achieved. Thanks to the lodge worker, food court waiter and the Thane police.

This concludes case history inputs by TLF

An Imaginative Journey of the Reality

Part 3

Duars Expressmail

Duars Expressmail is named so, for a specific reason. It is a small but effective foundation for the cause of anti human trafficking. It was founded in

The few case stories recorded here with changed names are contributions from Duars Expressmail.

The eight states of North East [NE] India are among the most scenic, least polluted and most pleasant regions of India compared to other states except Kashmir and Himachal. Yet, the geographic advantages, low economy, lack of literacy and other vulnerabilities have caused some parts of the NE to be infested by traffickers.

Raj Bahadur Thapa [name changed] is an active independent activist determined to hunt down traffickers and rescue of their slaves closer to West Bengal [WB], Bangladesh and Nepal on the western side of NE India that's famous for most of the reported and unreported human trafficking cases of India. The capital of WB - Kolkata [formally Calcutta] has the biggest and most notorious red light area in India called Sonagachi. Kolkata has the busiest railway terminus in the country named Howrah; it can presently hold 23 trains with 24 coaches each in its terminus that connects to all states of India. The footfall of Howrah station is the highest in the country followed by Mumbai's train terminus called CST.

The land borders of Nepal are easily accessible with roads, forests and hill terrains to the states of UP [Uttar Pradesh] and Sikkim; while Bangladesh is closely bordered with WB. Other nearby states in the North East has land borders with Tibet, China, Bhutan and Myanmar. Nepal and Bangladesh are still developing countries and most used by traffickers. Their rural population is high; rate of literacy is low just as it is in UP, Bihar, Jharkhand, WB and NE generally. A majority of the rural population are economically backward, thus they are fertile grounds for traffickers. Nepal is the oldest source for sex traffickers; since decades they have transported and sold victims to RLAs of Indian cities.

3A. Trafficker in disguise of a Holy Man

A church pastor visited Raj Bahadur one evening to seek help in tracking down a missing girl of one of his church members. He was told to advise the family to lodge a police complaint first. The 12 year old Misty was a local school girl in the dusty town of Siliguri of north WB close to Sikkim and Nepal. Raj Bahadur visited the missing girls' house and looked around for clues and loopholes. He found a backdoor connected to Misty's bedroom. Beneath her bed he found two large magnets painted in different colors. He quietly stole those magnets for the purpose of investigation. The next day, he called Misty's parents for a meeting at his office. The two magnets were visibly placed on the side of his desk. The parents asked him "where did he get those magnets from?" He replied that those magnets belong to his friend and he did not know what it was used for. Misty's parents said that they had the same magnets and it was used to get relief from joint pain problems. During the meeting, he asked many questions about Misty, her friends, relatives and visitors. He learnt that a few days ago a stranger dressed as a young sadhu [Hindu holy man] visited their house pretending to sell magnets. He gave the reference of the local religious leader in the city, so he was welcomed. He was friendly and asked to be seated in the house. He asked for a glass of water and sold the magnets to them at a low reasonable price. He noticed Misty and cheerfully talked to her, asking her name and school details. After a short while, before he left, he asked to use the washroom. During his washroom visit, he walked up to the open backdoor of the house which led to an accessible street.

Raj Bahadur got suspicious when he heard that, he went back to the house to check the backdoor and the street it led to.

The next evening after Misty was reported missing; Raj Bahadur got a call from one of his team members that a friend from the nearby city of New Jalpaiguri had informed him about hearing sounds of a young boy crying from within a small locked house. The friend said that through the window of the house the crying child looked like a boy but she sounded like a girl! They reached the spot immediately with the police and found out that the crying child was gone.

New Jalpaiguri [NJP] is a railway junction that serves as a main station to connect to Siliguri, Darjeeling, Sikkim, Kolkata and other main stations of the Indian Railways network.

Raj Bahadur connected the dots of his suspicion and went to the police; they soon met with the local religious leader in the city and got the contact number of the magnet salesman identified as Indar, originally from the state Haryana bordering New Delhi. The next day they tracked down details of the number and its present location pointed to the town of Azamgarh in the state of Bihar 690 KM from NJP.

Raj Bahadur reported the case to SSB [a NGO against trafficking in Siliguri] who were close to Siliguri Police. They asked Raj Bahadur to reach Azamgarh and report to the police authority there. When Raj Bahadur and the Azamgarh police raided the tracked location of Indar, they were shocked to see Indar and Misty naked. Indar was caught red handed about to rape her! He was beaten up by the angry reactions of police in his nudity! He was captured in camera footage meant to serve as evidence. Unfortunately there was no lady member in the raid team [as per rules, there should be at least one].

While Indar was handled by the police, Raj Bahadur immediately wrapped up the girl in a bed sheet and comforted her with assurance of safety and restoration. They got her dressed and took her directly for medical tests. Fortunately they reached just in time before her hymen was torn by Indar. Investigations revealed that Indar lured her from the backdoor of her house while the parents were at work, he took her to NJP, kept her at his temporary rented house, trimmed her hair short and dressed her up to look like a boy, then he drugged her with sedatives and boarded the night train to Azamgarh. From there he planned to transport Misty to be sold to a brothel in Delhi.

The case was strong enough to be presented before the court. Siliguri police officers were called to testify. Raj Bahadur made sure that there were no delays to process that. Soon after a case of crime and arrest the case has to be presented to the court within 24 hours. A special court remains open on holidays. In the first hearing of the court, the court ordered the police to hand over the child to the parents through Raj Bahadur based on the parent's telephonic agreement.

Indar did not have a defense lawyer. The court passed the judgment sentencing him to seven years of RI [rigorous imprisonment]. RI was added to the sentence since the victim was a child. The Siliguri police commented that seven years of RI was not enough for a criminal like Indar.

During the first court hearing, Raj Bahadur was complimented by the Azamgarh magistrate for a job well done and later facilitated by the WB senior police officers at Siliguri for effective investigations.

3 B. Blessed to be a Blessing

Embraced by the majestic Himalayan range of mountains on its north, Nepal on its west, Bhutan on its east and West Bengal on the south, is Sikkim, the scenic state of north east India. Sikkim's capital Gangtok is a city frequented by tourists and is known to be among the beautiful cities of India. Close to Gangtok is the famous hill station – Darjeeling, another masterpiece of the Creator. Siliguri is the nearest base station for air and rail connections to the rest of India.

This is a miraculous story of Jhanvi, a survivor who was trafficked at the age of 12, escaped from a traffickers home when she was 14 and rescued 12 years after she was reported missing! As a child she lived as a single child of a widow in a small village by the riverside not far from Darjeeling.

In March 2018, my working partner to counter sex trafficking, Raj Bahadur would get Facebook messenger texts from Jhanvi for a few nights in the odd hours between 12 and 2 AM. In her texts, Jhanvi repeatedly asked for his help to get her back home to her mother. She never remembered her hometown address; she never knew the address of the place she was texting from. All she knew was that Bangalore was the city she was texting him from. After a few days Raj Bahadur got her number traced to a location in Bangalore which is more than 2500 kilometers by road from Gangtok!

Raj Bahadur found out the address of a Nepali family from West Bengal living at Bangalore. They were related to his friend in Siliguri. He contacted them requesting a visit appointment without mentioning the actual purpose. He was called by them. Meanwhile he talked to Jhanvi and told her that he would be visiting Bangalore to find her. He asked her how she landed there. She told him that she was brought by a woman and kept with a man in a private flat 12 years ago. Raj Bahadur suspiciously figured out a case of trafficking.

Raj Bahadur set out on his train journey of 50 hours to Bangalore. He visited the Nepali family there and talked to them seated in the living room and said that he was there to look for a missing girl. They told him that he can go around and check. He got their contact number and traced its location. He was excited to know that the location matched with Jhanvi's number. Raj Bahadur stepped out of their house and messaged Jhanvi to inform him that he was in Bangalore. To his amazement, she replied that she was inside in the bedroom of the same house he had visited! Raj Bahadur did not go to the local police. He went back to the Nepali family's house to find Jhanvi. He spoke to her and got clues of the name of her village in Darjeeling. Raj Bahadur called up his elder son and told him to go to the local police station there and allow the officer to speak to him. Raj got the confirmation about the missing girl report filed at his police station in 2005. Raj told the police that he has found the girl and will be bringing her back to Darjeeling. The police in excitement cooperated with him and broke the good news to Jhanvi's lonely depressed mother.

Meanwhile, Raj Bahadur spoke to Jhanvi. She had mixed feelings of joy as she tearfully confided in him saying that she was tricked and drugged by the woman in Gangtok. She was mostly asleep on the train journey to Bangalore.

The woman handed over her to her buyer and left. She was traumatized as she was raped often by the monstrous buyer and his friends. After two years of enslavement and abuse she managed to escape from that man's apartment. Looking pale and lonely, perhaps affected by PTSD, she was spotted by a group of Nepali youth with a friendly stray dog sitting on the steps of a closed store. She was an innocent 14 year old then. The youth spoke her language, treated her food and helped her to move to the Nepali family who was known to them. The family sheltered her. Unfortunately, none of them reported to the Bangalore police. Had they done so, the criminals who enslaved her and the woman who trafficked her would be arrested and convicted.

A helpful boy from the youth group returned to visit Jhanvi a few years later, he gifted her a new mobile phone and kept in touch. He looked up on Google for NGOs and activists in the Siliguri-Darjeeling-Gangtok areas. He got Raj Bahadur's number and passed it on to Jhanvi - better late than never.

The Nepali family were a working couple, they had school going kids. They used Jhanvi as a maid and treated her well with food and comfort. 12 years had passed; Jhanvi's poor mother in Darjeeling had given up finding her daughter after frantic searches. She spent days and nights thinking about her daughter.

Before they could leave Bangalore, Raj spoke to the Nepali family telling them that it was illegal for them to keep her for 12 years. It was as good as imprisonment. Had they reported to the police, Jhanvi and her mother would not have to wait for so many years to be reunited. Upon Jhanvi's arrival, the Darjeeling police welcomed her and complemented Raj Bahadur for his efforts. They soon investigated to find and find her trafficker. A few days they learnt that her trafficker had committed suicide 10 years ago to avoid arrest by the Sikkim police hounding her for trafficking local girls. The man who bought Jhanvi then for 35000 rupees [about $ 800 then] in 2005 was not to be found as the police could not get the seller alive.

Jhanvi and her mother were overjoyed to be united and so were the villagers. A few years later Jhanvi moved to work as a maid with a rich family in the city of Rohtak about 2 hours away from Delhi. She is happy employed by them and visits her mother twice a year.

Jhanvi is still in contact with Raj Bahadur and cheerfully sends him a small monthly church donation of 100 rupees [$ 1.50] regularly every month. This amount is joyfully appreciated and received as a blessing as if its 1000 rupees!

Recently, as I hung up speaking to Jhanvi over the phone, I thought to myself, how blessed she is to be a blessing in the eyes of God.

3C. Carried away via Facebook

This is a very recent story of a group of survivors rescued by Nepal police coordinating with Raj Bahadur. An industrialist from Siliguri called up Raj to ask for help as he had been scammed online. He lost a big amount of money from his account due to cyber theft. On further questions he revealed that he was trapped by an online sex worker. She took the payment in advance for the appointment he had booked. With the help of the local police, her number was noted down and traced to a brothel in Siliguri. The name used to book the sim card was noted by Raj.

Raj pretended to be a prospective customer and called her. He said that he would not pay up in advance but he would pay up the amount at the time of the appointment. She gave him the address of an apartment and told him to call 10 minutes before he could reach. Raj informed the local police. They got details that girls were locked up in that apartment and forced to trap customers online. They were also forced to call customers at the same apartment for bedroom encounters.

Coincidentally the next day, Raj got a call form from an inspector of AHTU police in Nepal. The inspector asked if he could help to find a few missing Nepali girls. Raj asked for the photographs and names of the girls. Raj shared that information with six nearby police stations in north eastern India. Siliguri police found one name matching with the number at the online sex apartment. They contacted Raj to send decoy customers. All said and done….the raid was conducted and fourteen

Nepali girls were rescued from there. Three accused were arrested. All the girls were reported missing from Nepal. One girls name and number matched with the cyber theft complaint by Siliguri police. She was detained for questioning and revealed names of the two other accused on the run. Siliguri police was confident of getting them. Meanwhile the detained girl, Komal was released as a victim and handed over to Nepal police who had come to take the fourteen girls back.

On their road trip back to Kathmandu, the girls were given a short break by the side of the river bank bordering India and Nepal. Seven of them escaped across the summer dried river bed only to get caught by India's border guards. They were handed over to the local police and questioned. That police station verified details with Siliguri police and the Nepal police were informed.

The girls revealed that they were addicted to Facebook and were lured by good looking profiles of boys looking for partners with promises of a better future across the border in India soon after the lockdown ended in 2021. Their communications were in Nepali language that matches with many Nepali settlers in the Siliguri-Sikkim-Darjeeling region of North Eastern India.

The Nepal police picked up the rest of them to be transported back.

An Imaginative Journey of the Reality

Part 4

Rescue Foundation

Since the year 2000, more than 6000 lives have been saved, it has won nine awards from the President of India, organizations in the USA, Taiwan, and from Free a Girl, Netherlands…Rescue Foundation has four offices and shelter homes in India and is well known to fight for the cause to Counter Sex Trafficking in India and rebuild lives of survivors.

Recently during my visit to Rescue Foundation head office, I had a pleasant conversation with the co-founder Mrs. Triveni Acharya. She narrated the organizations story - here it is in her own words:

"I used to be a journalist, in the year 1993 I was instructed to go to Kamatipura, the red area in south Mumbai to note observations and submit a report. I was discouraged by one of my colleagues and asked to refuse. But, I insisted on going there on the day of the Hindu festival called 'Raksha Bandhan' [a day when women respect their brothers by tying colorful bands around their wrists.] a while later, I took a walk in one of the by lanes and noticed curtains on open ground level brothels. I entered one of them and came across small cubicles with a few girls lying down. I noticed a small girl who seemed under aged among other Nepali girls. I smiled and started to talk to them. I asked them if they go to school. One of them replied, no. I asked them where her parents were, and they replied that they were in Nepal, while we were here doing dirty work. They said that they were helpless, they were brought from Nepal and sold her, harassed and forced to work to restore the amount to the brothel keeper. I told them to run away. They said that they can't because they were pimps standing around in the street to catch them. So, then I said that I would help them to escape and reach home. After a short while the brothel owner came back from the street function she was attending, she questioned me about my identity. I told her that I was a journalist, she told me to leave, I did not argue, I left. ON my way back I was troubled in my thoughts. I recollected the days when I would see CSW's standing on the street and I used to think that they were doing their business voluntarily. I had no idea of human trafficking neither did the society and the police. Everyone was ignorant. But, I figured out that the girls were cheated, transported, sold and forced to be CSW's.

When I returned home I spoke to my husband and told him that innocent girls have been lured into slavery. He replied that he too needed to talk to me on this subject for a week. He said that there was a girl in the RLA who was infatuated with a boy working under me as a salesman. When the girl told her madam that she intends to marry this boy, she refused to let her go, she said that she had bought her for 50000 rupees and would not let her go as that money has to be recovered. The salesman requested my husband's help by saying that since your wife is a journalist, she may have some contacts with the police to help solve the problem. We decided to rescue this victim as well as the girls I met with. I told my husband to go along with the salesman to the Nagpada police station within the jurisdiction of the RLA. Meanwhile I contacted the CID office at the police headquarters. When the police team went to rescue that one victim about 15 others requested to be rescued as well! At that time we were using pagers, and I had got a page from my husband, he said that he was interested in rescuing the other girls too. At my request the local police station got a call to co-operate from the headquarters. They managed to rescue the girls but did not lodge an FIR (first information report) as SOP's of trafficking were not in place those days. They just rescued the victims without arresting the accused traffickers. They girls were officially recorded as lost and found homeless! The police sarcastically told us that since we were thrilled about doing social service, we would rather take the victims to our home. So, we took them home. Since they were all from Nepal, we took them there. Some of them didn't know their address. There was a shelter home that was run by a NGO called Maitri Nepal. In India shelter homes did not exist. Police used to record cases differently. We managed to repatriate most of them to their families. The ones who could not be reunited with their families were handed over to Maitri Nepal's shelter home. Maitri Nepal agreed to accept more rescued victims from us. They asked us if we can merge with them. Those days in India most slaves were from Nepal or from the North Eastern part of India. We merged with Maitri Nepal and registered our organization in India as Maitri Nepal, India. We continued our work of rescuing slaves till we formed our own Rescue Foundation in the year 2000. My husband Balkrishna was an ex army man. He started his own business after his discharge from the army. Later, he gave up his business and asked me to continue as a journalist which I did until his tragic death in 2005. He was very active in the cause to counter sex trafficking. I took over in 2005. Till date we have rescued more than 6000 victims."

4 A. The Missed Train

Sapna, a poor innocent child, lived with her family in a mud house thatched with dried palm leaves in a remote village of West Bengal. Her father, like any other struggling farmer focused on his crops, would be depending on the weather and worried about those destroyers among insects, birds and animals. Sapna school education ended at grade 4. Unlike America, free government schooling in India is too limited with seats mostly full. Life was hard for Sapna and her family; she had to cope up with demands to complete household responsibilities as well as assisting her father with farming. Agricultural work can be tedious and mentally stressful in many parts of India to those who cannot afford to invest in machinery, labor and fertilizers. There has been a high rate of farmer suicides in India in the last few decades. Reason for most suicides is depression. Reasons for depression for most farmers are failed harvest, weather disturbances or pressure from the bank to repay loans.

One fateful day in the year 2003, the sixteen year old Sapna and her eighteen year old cousin sister Deepa decided to go for a day break. They planned to venture around the city of Kolkata. They had left for the nearby city by train. Too much of excitement caused them to forget about the train timings to return back. They missed the evening train. It was late and the next train to their village would leave some unsuitable hours later. They were scared and worried as they had no alternatives. Their poverty status at that time made telephonic communications with the family impossible.

Their nightmare began when two women traffickers approached them with sweetness and kindness while they were seated at the station corner with faces hung down in despair. The evil intended women showed much kind concern and offered them to spend the night at their house. The girls were told that they could catch the morning train and travel safely back to their village. The poor girls got convinced as usual.

Sapna and Deepa gladly followed the two elderly witches to their last peaceful night together. The next morning, the witches added a magic potion to their breakfast. The innocent beings were sedated and prepared for transportation.

Sapna regained consciousness in an auto rickshaw [Tuk Tuk] rolling its tiny 3 wheels on the rough roads of Pune city 34 hours away by express train [east to west of India.] Sapna found herself with one of the witches and Deepa was missing. She cried as fear of the unknown has seeped in her innocence. The dizzy effect of a strong dose of magic portion was still affecting her.

Sapna's expected destination was a brothel house. She was caged. The awful phase of coercion, verbal and physical abuse had begun as Sapna refused to comply with their demands. As usual she was starved until that phase ended with her helpless submission to those slave runners.

Six months later, Sapna was transferred to another branch of the Pune RLA. She was a forced victim of sex slavery for years. She desperately made many attempts to get clues of her cousin Deepa. She often imagined ways to escape back but dreaded with fear and guilt of being held responsible for losing Deepa.

Sapna reached a point of accepting her destiny as a forced slave and had given up hopes to reunite with her family. It was time for the prayers of her parents to be answered. It was time for a breakthrough.

In June 2014, Rescue Foundation teamed up with the Pune Police and opened the gates of freedom to 21 forced victims of sex slavery in the Pune RLA. For Sapna it was like getting freed from a prison sentence of almost 12 years.

In every raid, the police cannot earn credits without getting some accused charged with crimes sex trafficking. Six of them were charged.

The victims were sheltered by the Rescue Foundation. Post court orders to repatriate them, partner NGOs in West Bengal gathered information that Sapna's parents had filed a missing report in 2003. They reached out to Sapna's parents to reconfirm Sapna's identity and willingness to accept her. Sapna's mother had conditioned herself that her daughter had died, so it took a while for her to believe Sapna's existence.

NGO partners in Kolkata escorted Sapna's mother to travel to Pune. At the shelter home she was so shocked to see her daughter, that she grabbed her daughter's cheeks, looked into her tearful eyes and asked her questions of her childhood. Both of them held on to each other in a long tearful embrace. Soon later they were assisted with requirements to travel back comfortably to Kolkata.

Sadly, Deepa remains missing with no clues about her, a burden of regret for Sapna to live with. The two witches of Kolkata were never tracked down by the police as many years had passed.

4 B. Lifeguards in an ocean of Sharks

Jyoti was born and brought up in West Bengal. Her father was a driver and his earnings were not enough to support his family. Somehow, he managed to let Jyoti study in school till grade 10th. She was seventeen. She failed her final exams and that discouraged her to continue further. Her parents couldn't afford to keep her in school anymore.

It was the summer of 2017. Soon their financial burdens got heavier as Jyoti's mother fell sick and had to undergo surgery for removal of kidney stones. Her father made many failed attempts to borrow money from people in order to collect the funds needed for the surgery. Unfortunately he met an acquaintance called Aslam who told him about job prospects for Jyoti as an upper class domestic help in the city of Mumbai. He offered her father money if he agreed to send Jyoti. He said that he had another girl called Babli who had also agreed to accept the offer. He said that he needed one more girl. Since he was desperately in need of money, he agreed. He took Aslam home to introduce him to Jyoti and explained to her to join Aslam to work in Mumbai. Though Jyoti was not comfortable with the offer, she thought about her mother's surgery expenses and compromised to accept the offer. She packed her belongings and left with them on the journey of deception.

Jyoti and Babli [also seventeen] were dropped at a location on the outskirts of Mumbai. They were totally ignorant of the new places as they trusted Aslam. They were handed over to a woman who kept them for a day and then led them to Pune by train. Sadly, their destination was a building in Budhwar Peth, the RLA of Pune.

As soon as they reached the destination, the girls got suspicious and felt uncomfortable about the environment. The brothel keeper told them that she had paid for them and arrogantly explained the job they had to do.

The girls were shocked and filled with fear. They begged the brothel keeper with joined hands to let them go. The manager yelled at them with verbal abuses and threatened them to comply as there was no other way out.

Both girls were then pushed into the honeymoon suites specially designed for the highest bidder to sleep with virgins. Even before the customer could arrive in the first hour, the terrified girls heard a commotion outside the suite rooms. The brothel keeper approached them in panic and demanded them not to say a word to the police who were there on a surprise raid.

Based on a tip off from a reliable source, the Rescue Foundation team pursued the Pune AHTU police to urgently conduct a surprise raid. The women police team noticed the fearful faces of Jyoti and Babli and pulled them out from the sharks infested zone.

11 other forced victims were rescued from that brothel. The brothel keeper was charged as the main accused. Two pimps were arrested. Within a short time, the transporter from Mumbai was arrested by Mumbai police and handed over to Pune police. Aslam was arrested in Kolkata and handed over to the Pune police who filed a strong charge sheet to the court for severe conviction of all accused.

The victims were sheltered by the Rescue Foundation. Jyoti and Babli were the first ones to be safely repatriated to their families. The informer was secretly rewarded.

The Pune AHTU team was praised for swift actions. The Rescue Foundation team submitted a praise report and a letter of gratitude to the Commissioner of Police. This was a case of victory for both rescue teams.

4 C. Caterpillar to Butterfly

Transformation of a Survivor

Nepal, so economically backward that most of its population is still affected with poverty. Because of its mountain terrains and unsuitable climatic conditions, industrialization is just as limited as agriculture is. The nation depends mainly on income from tourism and mountaineering. Enthusiatic men tourists generally increase the market demand for sex. This is the reason why supply of commercial sex has escalated in Katmandu and now in some parts of Goa, India.

Tina was originally from Nepal. Her impoverished parents passed away when she was just an 8 year old child. Her elder sister Rina worked as a daily wage laborer to make ends meet. Three years later Rina got into a relationship, got married and left to live with her husband.

Rina wanted to take her along but her uncle refused to allow her. He kept Tina at his place where she was not allowed to go to school and was ill-treated by the uncle's wife. Two years later, Tina felt frustrated and left their house. She went to the place where her sister used to work and met with a familiar lady who helped get a job and room to live along with her.

She stayed with the lady peacefully for about 7 months. At work she got infatuated with a boy working together. They fell in love, and she decided to accept his proposal to marry. She was just 15, a very immature, illiterate teenager.

Trusting her boyfriend's plans, she decided to leave with him. A few days later, she got paid off her dues from the good lady who had helped her and they left for a town called Nepalgunj which was a 24 hour bus journey. From there they made a short trip to Lucknow, the capital of UP state in India. In a short time, they left by train to Nasik, a small city on the way to Mumbai, about 20 hours away. At Nasik they stayed at a lodge, where they got physically intimate. Her boyfriend convinced her of a better future and promised to get married.

Later, the boy whom she was in love with took her to a place called Badrakali, the RLA of Nasik. On the street there he asked her to wait at a particular spot and promised to return. She waited for him all day. He was gone. She felt lost, hungry, tired, insecure and abandoned as the dusk settled.

Even though she was uneducated, she observed the seductive uncleanness in the unusual atmosphere around. Women were scantily dressed and were being approached by swaying men in drunken states. A sense of loneliness quickly shot up to surface her conscience. Later at night, she sat in a corner with a nervous breakdown and began crying helplessly. A woman approached her, listened to her sad story and offered her place to rest. She helplessly agreed to that offer. She was too hurt and betrayed by the boy she loved and trusted, she was broken hearted and slipped into depression. The woman sheltered her and provided food for a few days while she tried to figure out what to do with Tina. The woman was not a trafficker. A few days later, as Tina settled down, the woman confided her story to Tina. Without coercion and abuse she encouraged Tina to sell her body and earn a living.

Tina's world changed as she worked there. Three years later she was rescued by the police who contacted her elder sister Rina, who came to take custody of her. That was in June 2016. Meanwhile Rina's husband used to regularly fight and there was no peace at home. Tina was frustrated and called up a friend who used to work as a sex worker. Tina left to join her friend at Nandurbar.

She worked there for 2 years till she was rescued again. This time by the Rescue Foundation's biggest [at that time] rescue operation teamed up with Maharashtra Police. Together they rescued 67 girls among which 17 were minors.

Tina was sheltered at the Rescue Foundation's well equipped shelter home at Boisar. In the beginning, she was full of collective anger and refused to participate in any educational and constructive activities. She was too pessimistic about her future life.

Counselors and social workers did not give up on her, soon they began molding and shaping her to be a new woman. They achieved results in their hard work as Tina showed good results in overall activities and training. She was gradually groomed to carry herself with dignity. She was trained to speak and communicate well with others. All of the inmates who go through the process of cleansing streams forget about using verbal abuse. They learn to give and take respect from others. They learn to open up to the true practice of love and kindness.

Within 2 years she progressed to join an e-commerce store where she received training in tailoring and jewelry making. She earned a stipend there for a year till the time of completion.

Rescue Foundation trained her to be a receptionist and is proud to place her at the head office. Tina's job involves business telephonic communications with external contacts and internal staff, welcoming guests, setting up appointments, key's management, making notes in registers and data entries.

During the lockdowns she conducted art and dance classes for the newer survivors.

She has taken up a leadership position of being a good example setter and is respected by all the survivors at RF shelter homes.

The diverse parts of her story of being orphaned, uneducated, of hard labor, betrayal and transformation remain a testimony to inspire her sister and all other survivors sheltered in all the homes of Rescue Foundation. Compliments to the efforts of the RF counselors and social workers for a job well done.

4 D. Minor saved just in Time

There are a few villages in the states of Rajastan and MP that are known for traditional commercial sex work. Betul is one such town in MP popular for escort services and online publicity of the availability of sex workers. These are markets that need to be monitored as the possibility of forced sexual exploitation and trafficking cannot be ruled out.

The following information is excerpted from a report by Indiatimes dated 2013.

"Sex is our family business," says Manju Thakur, 30, who's zealously protective of what to her is a lucrative livelihood. Diminutive but feisty, the sex worker is a Bedia, a lower caste community in Rajasthan and Madhya Pradesh, where young girls, often in their teens, engage in prostitution with the consent of the community.

Plying the only trade she knows from the profusely littered roadside near Bharatpur's Malaha village, Manju is a veteran. "I was just about 10 or 11 years old when my father, who is dead now, sent me to a well-off businessman in Dhaulpur," she says, appearing almost nostalgic recalling the Rs 10,000 her family received in exchange for her loss of virginity. "Twenty years ago, it was the maximum any girl was paid for here," she says, also proudly informing you how "rich customers from Jaipur " still come by asking for her.

"Dhanda chokha hai (Business is good)," Manju smiles, reapplying her lipstick in anticipation of another temporary suitor. Manju and her sisters Nisha, 25, and Reshma, 24, as well as their 20-year-old bua (aunt) Chandani supports

a family of 40 including five brothers, their wives, their children and a brood of offspring from the trade.

Source - https://www.indiatoday.in/magazine/society-the-arts/story/20131028-sex-trade-and-tradition-family-business-bedia-families-768084-1999-11-30

Monica was raised in the Bedia community of Rajasthan. She was a fortunate teenager not pushed into the family business at 16. She was aware that someday it would be her turn as he often witnessed her aunt and her mother entertaining men. She was conditioned to believe that this would be her career too.

Monica was a school girl earlier till she was forced to give up on education as her mother had financial problems to afford it.

One day in March 2019, they traveled to the city of Mumbai and stayed at an aunt's house. A few days later, a group of girls working at a dance bar visited the aunt's house. They convinced Monica if she would be interested as their work involved dancing only. Since she had no other options to earn, she agreed. She did well there and was satisfied with her job of just dancing. She lasted till the bar closed down due to the first lockdown. She and her mother were among those daily wage workers who slipped into poverty during the lockdowns. They had to deal with food shortage.

Sujit was a pimp looking for money making opportunities. He was known to Monica's aunt and visited their place one day in the lockdown. He told Monica's mother that there were new customers available to pay a good price for young girls like her daughter. The desperate mother believed him and agreed to his offer to a meeting with the clients.

The Rescue Foundation investigation team received a tip off of this meeting from an informer. The police were quickly informed and a decoy customer was sent to Sujit and convinced him that he was willing to pay a high price for a virgin. Sujit was excited about the big money during lockdown. He brought Monica along. The decoy customer ordered beers and shared it, as he had to waste some time in order to give more prep time for the raid team. Meanwhile the image of the victim Monica was sent to confirm that she was a minor.

The RF raid team and police teams barged in moments later. Sujit was arrested and Monica was saved before she could lose her virginity into the dark world of prostitution. She was sheltered as ordered by the CWC. She was not allowed to join her mother back again at her home town. A decent job with food and comfortable accommodation was arranged for her later. That's where she is now, working as a domestic help for a respectable family.

4 E. Police Saviors

Mulund, Mumbai 2016 - Neha, a slum child lost both her parents at an early age of 8. She was taken care of by her grandparents, who were old and could barely afford her expenses. The only earning member was her mother's sister, working as a sex worker and diagnosed as HIV positive.

Neha was a happy playful normal child, she had many friends around. Somehow her grandparents managed to look after her. One of her close friends had her birthday coming up soon and had plans to treat the others at the nearby McDonalds. Neha was excited. Her cruel aunt heard about the kid's excitement about going to McDonalds. So, she made up an evil plan to trap the child. The news of her plan leaked out to an informer of the Rescue Foundation.

Her aunt approached Neha to invite her to another treat at the McDonalds on the same day. Neha refused as she preferred to join her friends. On her friend's birthday, Neha was preparing and was eagerly looking forward to it. Unfortunately a few hours later, the friend's party was canceled causing much disappointment to Neha.

Her aunt made use of the opportunity and set up the trafficker's appointment at McDonalds. Neha was cheered up and convinced about getting treated at the restaurant by her aunt.

Soon as they entered McDonalds they were met with two men hosting the treat. One of the men asked the 11 year old Neha to go check out what she would like to eat while her aunt started dealing with the men.

To counter the game plan, one of the two men was an undercover decoy customer. He pretended to be busy chatting and sent messages from his phone.

Mulund police station is just about 1.5 KMs away from the McDonalds on the west. Within a short time, the police raid team arrived along with RF team and arrested her aunt and the pimp.

The loss of a tender childhood of an innocent girl was prevented by effective support of the police. She was soon repatriated to her grandparents. The police team pooled in a donation amount to open a fixed deposit account in the bank for Neha which would be useful for her future when she would turn 18. A separate cash donation was given to her grandparents. In addition to all those gestures of kindness, the police helped the child to get admitted in a free municipal school nearby and finally McDonalds invited her for a free treat along with her 5 friends!

Now wasn't that a good move of kindness.

Prevention points to
Counter Sex Trafficking

1. Preventive measures young women need to be aware of about traffickers

Providing information and education regarding deceptive manipulation techniques used to lure young girls should be part of a constant awareness program. Social media messenger apps can to be used to educate girls on awareness of trafficking. Institutions and women's organizations must initiate programs to do so. Senior police and border security authorities must implement stringent actions against corrupt lower level staff that support crimes of trafficking just for their own satisfaction of greed. Instead they could be awarded for reporting and initiating arrest of traffickers. The law enforcements should work out systems and strategies to catch, warn and persecute customers before they make demands from traffickers. Traffickers will lose business to supply when the customer demand is less. This is simple marketing economics.

Primary websites utilized by sex traffickers in the United States from 2015 to 2020

https://www.statista.com/statistics/978966/primary-websites-used-sex-traffickers-us-number-cases/

Traffickers abusing online technology, UN crime prevention agency warns https://news.un.org/en/story/2021/10/1104392

US Human Trafficking and Social Media
https://polarisproject.org/human-trafficking-and-social-media/

US Department of Justice – Child Trafficking
https://www.justice.gov/criminal-ceos/child-sex-trafficking

https://www.businessinsider.in/tech/news/facebook-was-used-to-recruit-victims-in-more-than-half-of-sex-trafficking-cases-in-2020-according-to-a-new-report/articleshow/83407180.cms

Traffickers usually disguise themselves to operate as any character - a husband and wife couple; as an elderly lady or man; or a rich young girl or boy. They are well programmed with what to talk and how to behave. They usually carry some kind of material that will influence the prospective victim. They can show the prospect impressive images or videos on their mobile. They can even show up fake images of themselves standing alongside celebrities. Some traffickers trap girls by showing them their impressive offices or residences. They can offer the prospect a good treat in a good restaurant. They can be helpful with a financial tip or gift. They can operate by approaching the prospects parents and brain washing them first. This is usually done by familiar acquaintances, relatives or referred by relatives in poverty stricken regions.

Do not believe in sweet talks of bragging strangers. Do not get carried away by the kindness of unknown men or women who have an over friendly or helpful approach towards you. They could be dressed up in a religious outfit.

Do not get easily flattered with praises about your own looks, physical appearance, clothing, pets, jobs, family, etc.

Do not get easily influenced by a stranger's business card, expensive vehicle, electronic gadgets, appearance, clothing and style

Do not believe in everything strangers say and do not accept a ride, treat, food or drinks from them

Do not answer questions or disclose details about your personal goals, personal or family problems, personal drawbacks or weaknesses to unknown persons

Do not give your contact numbers, address or personal details to unknown persons

Do not agree to go along with them and do not allow them to accompany or follow you back home

Do not communicate with unknown people by any means of social media platforms and apps. Do not answer questions and respond to unknown people on the phone. Do not give out information about your daughters, sisters or friends. Do not get influenced by appealing pop up's on the internet and respond to them

Do not reply or send details to fraudulent mails from unknown sources. Scam before opening

Do not give photographs or allow anyone [even women] to shoot your still or video photographs

Do not mention your desires to go abroad, to get into films or modeling or to get a highly paid job

Do not get convinced by anyone to help you with money, job offers or opportunities in films, TV serials, advertisements, modeling, airline jobs, jobs in big cities, highly paid jobs, business offers or foreign trips

Do not have negative thoughts, panic or fear of threats or revenge attacks if you have to inform the police and in any event of a trafficker's movements, please report by calling the emergency number, sending a tweet or a message to the police control room

In most developing countries reporting to police control rooms works more effectively than calling the local police station. The local police could be corrupt.

The light shines in the darkness, and the darkness has not overcome it - John 1:5ohn 1:

2. Young women be your own bodyguard

Points on Self-Security

Women are known to be protected by common universal rights in democratic countries. Generally they enjoy better safety and respect in advanced cultures and limited privileges in conservative cultures. They have been targets of honor killing, discrimination, abuse and suffering in less liberated cultures of the world. For example, laws in Iran are getting extremely cruel towards women. Saudi Arabia have restrictions and limitations for women to enjoy freedom. Iran now is getting closer to being over conservative. while Afghanistan is the most difficult nation for women since Taliban took over. Recently

Saudi Arabia has allowed them to drive cars! The rest of the GCC countries like Oman and particularly United Arab Emirates have been more respectful and lenient towards them. In the last two decades, many unreported cases of sexual, physical and mental abuse of foreign maids in Kuwait have been leaked out as much as they are prevalent, possibly the highest among the oil rich states there. Embassies of the Philippines, India, Bangladesh and Sri Lanka have made shelters to accommodate runaway maids before they could be deported.

In developing countries women are known to be victims of various kinds of abuse for reasons of being physically weaker and mentally ignorant. They are suppressed and forced to be submissive to the husband as per traditional rules laid out by their religious beliefs and caste systems. In regions where slavery is present, women are exploited to forced labor in agriculture, fashion and mining industries. CNN Freedom reports that slavery in fashion industry is booming in Bangladesh, which is well known for garment export market.

While women can enjoy the freedom to carry themselves safely in developed parts of the world, the less fortunate ones in developing countries can save themselves from being abused or attacked if they practice self-security measures on a daily basis. Women have been targets of sexual crimes, physical abuse, forced labor and acid attacks. India is on the list of countries where crimes against women is on the highest. Some crimes go unregistered and unreported due to coercion ,threats and blackmail. Statistics of crimes released by any government cannot be accepted as complete.

Know your Rights as a Woman in your own country

The following points will be necessary for girls/women in vulnerable places:

• Rights as a woman for dignity and respect that implies no male of any age has the right to sexually harass her verbally or physically

• As respect under all circumstances, no one has the right to make women uncomfortable, whether at work place, home, on the streets, in institutions or in a social gathering

• Rights to physical and mental security. No one has the rights to use physical force, torture [physically or mentally] a woman no matter whoever it is in relationship with the victim

• Privilege to complain - Women have all the rights to complain when violated even in the least way. Women can decide to use the correct means of law in such circumstances, whatever the status of the offender is — boss, relative, or politician

• Rights as a women employee must be on the notice board/rules as per the set guidelines for prevention of sexual harassment at workplaces

• Abuse of women is not her fate as it is taken for

granted in some places. Intimidated behavior is not a woman's destiny, thus reporting against it must be done as early as possible

Common tips applicable to women:

● Women should be concerned about their own security especially during vulnerable times [at night] and at crime infested sensitive locations

● A woman's mental strength is more important than physical power. Develop a strong will, eye movements like an alert ferocious dog and a commanding voice to resist possible advances by prowling two legged hyenas

● Build up an instinct to sense danger and make no mistakes

● Challenging weather and lonely late night darkness are vulnerable times for any woman

● Isolated places increase level of vulnerability. These can be corners, dead end streets, buildings, bridges, parking lots, staircases or even lifts

● Escaping from a possible attack scenario is more sensible than confronting it. A cat has nine lives because it skillfully escapes death eight times

● Maintain physical fitness, be active and avoid consumption of any kind of intoxication

Measures young women should take to prevent criminal attack:

Be alert and accept your vulnerability in any culture. Roll your eyes 360 degrees and your waist 180 degrees at random intervals. Keep your head up, stand or walk in areas that have people around and bright overhead lights. Be sensitive in your appearance and behavior. Avoid being drunk. Wear clothes and footwear that will help you run, or take off your shoes and run bare feet if you have to. Watch for suspicious men or women lurking nearby; let them know that you are alert and courageous. Avoid hitch hiking offers by strangers. Blow a loud whistle, shout, yell or wave to attract attention of saviors in case of a threat or encounter.

• Save emergency numbers on your phone especially when you travel by road or rail

• Download apps that send distress messages from your cell phones or send a tweet to the police or your friends

• Plan your outstation travel as to arrive at the destination during day light hours. In case of delays or night arrivals, call trusted acquaintances to pick you up

• Inform about your travel routes and plans particularly at night and stay connected with acquaintances informing them about your locations

• Inform office security staff and at home in the case of a breakdown of a car if you are the last passenger to be dropped

• Keep your vehicle in good condition to avoid a

breakdown before you travel

• While driving, keep a hammer in the glove compartment to break open the window in case of a being electronically locked in the car

• Equip your car with a torch, spare tire, tools and first aid kit when you are going long distance

• Lock your car from inside while traveling at night

• Hire cabs from standard travel companies from the hotels cab service. In case of booking other cabs, note the number plate before boarding and text it to at least two persons closest to you

• Check the safety and security arrangements when staying in a hotel room. Prefer rooms with electronic keys and know where the emergency alarms and exits are

• Be cautious in making new friends while traveling or at hotel events

• Use the elevator, instead of stairs in a building. Avoid the elevator if its occupied by a suspicious person

• Leave the elevator in case a suspicious person gets in while you are alone

• Lock the doors of your house at all times and do not open the door to strangers. Install intercoms or video systems to speak to the stranger on the door

• Ensure proper lighting at the entrance to your house. The exit side should be at least 60 percent brighter than the entrance so that you are able to clearly see a person outside

• Communicate only with trusted acquaintances on social media. Don't trust people you don't know. Avoid making friends with them and don't get carried away by unknown sources

• Travel in women sections of trains or buses

• Carry items such as a whistle, pepper spray/red chili powder and a mini working flash light in your handbag

• Know weak areas of the male anatomy in case you have to attack these parts are mainly — groin, throat, eyes and knees

• Learn to use your elbow, knees and fingernails these are advantages of women to hurt when it strikes the right spots

• Learn to use PPCT [pressure point control tactics] from the internet

• If fond of pets, keep two guard dogs and take them out for together as they can be more agressive and effective as a team

• Dogs can sense bad strangers near the house or outside. They have always been helpful for security

• Educate your female students, neighborhood and daughters on this subject of self-security

Know what you are not supposed to do

• Do not hesitate to object to misbehavior the first time it happens. Ignoring it once will only encourage the offender to repeat it

• Do not venture to investigate alone and never in the late evenings

• Do not travel alone at night or even in a group of girls in cities of developing or religiously radicalized countries

• Do not travel in public transport alone, in case you find yourself alone in a train, move to sections that have more people or seek help from uniformed security or staff

• Do not join in protests or crowds unless you are in a group, molestation is common at such times

• Do not make unnecessary eye contact with strangers. Exchanging frequent glances can be misunderstood

• Do not engage in conversation with a stranger especially when you are alone

• Do not show unnecessary sympathy for a stranger; sometimes women decoys are used by criminals to lure female victims

• Do not set a routine of timings and routes while going out and returning, change your timings and routes as frequently as possible, in case you are in a unfamiliar area

• Do not hesitate to raise an alarm or to report any suspicious person, activities or object close to your residence

• Do not give up if you are under threat or attack, look for opportunity to escape

• Do not show fear, assailants are encouraged by the weakneses shown by their targets

• Do not use ATMs' at deserted spots and at times

• Do not carry all the money or your ID's in one place

• Do not wear expensive jewelry while travelling. Do not display it after the event or occasion is over

• Do not accept food or drinks from strangers

• Do not consume excessive alcohol or allow your male partner to do so. This exposes your vulnerability

• Do not drive after consuming alcohol nor allow your partner to do so

• Do not allow your social behavior to be out of control. Never greet strangers with a hug or a kiss

Take no part in the worthless deeds of evil and darkness; instead, expose them – Ephesians 5:11

Conclusion

This topic covers almost every detail of precautions and emergency measures by women to be taken with regards to their own safety. Among all men, a very small percentage can be regarded as nasty. 'It is better be safe than sorry' is most appropriately applied to women.

Advanced countries invest in better and wider police patrols in their cities. Rural places in those countries may not have access to public transport at night. Young women travelling alone at odd hours at remote places can be generally safe in advanced countries like North America, Europe, Japan, Australia and New Zealand. But not in South America, Africa, Middle East and developing countries in Asia even if public transport is available at night. If you have a male companion, you are less likely to be targeted, though there have been cases where the male companion or husband is physical attacked or killed.

https://www.youtube.com/watch?
v=SazZMIcxcws&ab_channel=JeffsonNathan

Reflect Light into the Dark
Side of the Earth

Modern slavery prevention strategies should be targeted towards young people to prevent exploitation from occurring. Recruitment tactics and methods of control used by exploiters would be much less effective if more information and support were readily accessible to young people - excerpted from UNSEEN report UK

Some years ago, I attended a 2 days seminar organized by the State Inspector General of Police. She had invited representatives from NGOs, police, CWC, judiciary, advocates and lawyers. All representatives were invited to submit topics to speak on. A few police officers shared the extreme cases of torture victims had to go through by traffickers who were narcissistic, perverts, maniacs, drugs or alcohol influenced evil men. They mentioned unimaginable torture done by methods of using burning cigarette ends, pricking needles or sharp nails into the pubic areas, breasts and buttocks of victims to terrify them so that they don't rebel. The traumatized effects of various forms of torture committed on victims are the same may it be in the US, Bosnia, Syria, Latin America, Africa, India and wherever. Such ultimate evil acts sourced by demonic influences are common worldwide because the one who is driving them is the same. This is what I believe, you may agree or not. Criminals influenced by demons are noted to be merciless, shameless, filthy, ugly, smelly, bizarre, brutal and horrific to levels beyond the definition of inhumane.

Through direct interaction with survivors, we have heard many diversified truthful and tearful submissions of the survivors we rescued. We learnt of the extremely distressing experiences they were caught up in right from every step of how they were deceived, recruited, abused, controlled, tortured, exploited and forced to be slaves. As they spoke to us, each one of them wished that no other girl should fall into the same trap and experience the same atrocities. I realized that if such a wish which cannot be fulfilled by them [in their helpless capacity] it can be fulfilled by us – that's you and me.

Has the information in this book edified you? If you have been moved by this imaginative journey of reality, I encourage you to do some more study, watch some movies and documentaries listed in this chapter. I encourage you to take some actions, make some efforts to shed light into areas of darkness. This is the way we can collectively bring the stormy wide and deep ocean of Sex Trafficking under control.

Please educate girls and women around you in constant programmed methods. I encourage:

- Associations of women to organize awareness programs in the urban cities and towns to encourage others to spread it to rural areas

- Educate the society to break the stigma attached to victims

- Women should be educating men; men should be educating men and the youth.... the message should reach out to discourage those who make specific demands from agents and pimps. Break the demand to break the supply. Discourage watching pornography as some of the characters could be forced victims.

- Law enforcement officers to take stringent disciplinary actions against corrupt subordinates

- Lawyers and judiciary to work for refusal of bails, severe convictions of traffickers and customers who make specific demands from them

- Industrialists and corporate to utilize funding budgets like CSR into setting up shelter homes of victims with visiting psychiatrists and counselors

- Movie makers to educate the public though movies in various languages. Movie makers to stop portraying commercial sex workers as prostitutes and start using the term 'victims' [of slavery] instead.

- Luxury hotels, lodges, motels and resort owners and general managers – stop selling your rooms to pimps. Clean up the contamination. Stick to pure hospitality business. Break the suppliers' access to guest rooms. Stop entry of escorts for special room service. Don't support the sex trafficking market to boom just to boost up your revenue. The seeds of trafficking sown are bound to reap a harvest that can reach your homes too.

Rescue the poor and helpless; deliver them from the grasp of evil people.
Rise up, O God, and judge the earth, for all the nations belong to you.
Psalm 82:4, 8, The Holy Bible, New Living Translation

For further edification

https://www.ice.gov/features/human-trafficking

https://www.cbsnews.com/news/facebook-sex-trafficking-online-recruitment-report/

https://www.state.gov/20-ways-you-can-help-fight-human-trafficking/

https://www.fbi.gov/investigate/violent-crime/human-trafficking

https://en.wikipedia.org/wiki/Cybersex_trafficking

- USA: Girl introduced to drugs, sold, used by politicians, priests, cops, dads, husbands, CEOs

https://www.youtube.com/watch?v=hf0QlC6oIeA&ab_channel=REALWOMEN%2FREALSTORIES

- USA: International Students trapped

https://thepienews.com/news/human-traffickers-target-international-students/

- USA: International Students trapped

https://thepienews.com/news/traffickers-exploiting-student-visas-at-global-level-reports-reveal/

- Canada: Toronto Students abused during the lockdowns

https://www.youtube.com/watch?
v=_TNuo6duAWY&ab_channel=PTCNews

- India: Award winning film 'AMOLI' – as short documentary in English on minor girls lured and sold

https://www.youtube.com/watch?
v=HGDEIjYg8s8&t=329s&ab_channel=BLUSH

- BBC report on trafficking Romanian girls

https://www.youtube.com/watch?
v=m12cgvH1R9w&ab_channel=BBCNews

- BBC report of Surviving Sex Trafficking 2020

https://www.youtube.com/watch?
v=ok_UO_vLN3Y&ab_channel=BBCNews

- Interview on introduction of the documentary Surviving Sex Trafficking March 2022

https://www.youtube.com/watch?
v=eUFQJz0H2I4&ab_channel=LRMOnline

https://thelogicalindian.com/exclusive/human-trafficking-africa-kenya-nigeria-sex-trade-bbc-documentary-19386

- Documentary - Stolen Innocence delves into a hidden world; the untold story of young women captured and forced into a life of sex slavery.

Without a choice, these girls are violently trafficked into the world's largest sex ring

https://www.youtube.com/watch?v=eTtBnPxNpYs&t=569s&ab_channel=StolenInnocence

Movies to watch on Sex Trafficking

- Trafficked – US story – American production 2017
- Eden – US story - American 2012

- Tricked – The Documentary – US story - American 2013

- Trade – Mexican story - American 2007

- Spartan – US story - American 2004

- The Whistleblower – Bosnian story – Canadian-American-German production 2010

- Eastern Promises – Russian British story – Canadian 2007

- Priceless – US story – American 2016

- The Storm Makers – Award winning documentary – Cambodian story – Cambodian French production 2014

- Born into Brothels - Award winning documentary – Indian [West Bengal story] – American 2004

- Amoli - Award winning documentary – Indian story – Indian 2019

- Girl Model – Russian Japanese story – American 2012

- Hope lost – Romanian Italian story – Italian 2015

- Surviving Sex Trafficking – Documentary – American March 2022

Surviving Sex Trafficking examines the ongoing struggles of those survivors as they desperately fight to break free of their past, heal their bodies and minds, reconnect with a world of hope, and reclaim their lost humanity. Jain monk Sadhvi Siddhali Shree, the filmmaker behind the award-winning documentary Stopping Traffic: The Movement to End Sex Traffic, uncovers the depth of pain felt by survivors as well as if and how they can truly recover. [Excerpted text]

The world of Human Trafficking at a glance - Please specifically read the paragraph on 'Trafficking Profile' of the US State Department reports

Philippines, Vietnam, Thailand, Cambodia, Hong Kong, Indonesia

https://pcij.org/article/6498/the-whole-internet-can-be-a-watchdog-how-to-fight-online-sex-abuse-of-children

https://pcij.org/article/6139/the-filipino-mothers-selling-their-children-for-online-sexual-abuse

https://www.bangkokpost.com/thailand/general/1447474/tourists-tapped-to-fight-human-trafficking

https://www.kent.ac.uk/news/society/26759/digital-serious-game-to-combat-online-child-sexual-exploitation-and-trafficking-in-thailand-and-cambodia

https://www.reuters.com/article/us-thailand-sexcrimes-internet-trfn-idUSKBN23P33K

https://www.state.gov/reports/2021-trafficking-in-persons-report/cambodia/

https://www.state.gov/reports/2021-trafficking-in-persons-report/vietnam/

https://www.state.gov/reports/2021-trafficking-in-persons-report/indonesia/

https://www.state.gov/reports/2021-trafficking-in-persons-report/hong-kong/

https://ijmhk.org/our-work/online-sexual-exploitation-of-children/

Sri Lanka, Bangladesh, Pakistan, Nepal,

Myanmar, Bhutan, Afghanistan

https://www.state.gov/reports/2021-trafficking-in-persons-report/sri-lanka/

https://www.state.gov/reports/2021-trafficking-in-persons-report/bangladesh/

https://www.hindustantimes.com/cities/lucknow-news/intl-human-trafficking-racket-over-200-women-from-myanmar-bangladesh-trafficked-101646156095323.html

https://techobserver.in/2021/06/21/bangladesh-criminals-leveraging-tiktok-to-lure-young-women/

https://www.cnn.com/2018/06/28/asia/human-trafficking-tip-report-myanmar-rohingya-intl/index.html

https://www.orfonline.org/expert-speak/myanmar-trafficking-issues-plight-rohingyas-thailand/

https://www.state.gov/reports/2021-trafficking-in-persons-report/pakistan/

https://www.theguardian.com/global-development/2018/jun/15/pakistan-shame-open-secret-child-sex-abuse-workplace-kasur

https://www.state.gov/reports/2021-trafficking-in-persons-report/bhutan/

https://www.state.gov/reports/2021-trafficking-in-persons-report/nepal/

https://www.researchgate.net/publication/344337212_Sex_Trafficking_In_Nepal_A_Review_of_Problems_and_Solutions

https://abcnews.go.com/Politics/wireStory/afghan-evacuation-raises-concerns-child-trafficking-79818599

https://www.youtube.com/watch?v=q5ZJt3hMdBQ

https://www.state.gov/reports/2021-trafficking-in-persons-report/afghanistan/

https://borgenproject.org/human-trafficking-in-afghanistan/

Iraq, Syria, UAE, Kuwait

https://www.state.gov/reports/2021-trafficking-in-persons-report/iraq/

https://borgenproject.org/human-trafficking-in-iraq/

https://www.state.gov/reports/2021-trafficking-in-persons-report/syria/

https://www.aljazeera.com/features/2020/2/11/the-syrian-women-and-girls-sold-into-sexual-slavery-in-lebanon

https://www.state.gov/reports/2021-trafficking-in-persons-report/united-arab-emirates/

https://borgenproject.org/human-trafficking-in-the-united-arab-emirates/

https://archive.dhakatribune.com/bangladesh/2020/09/12/dubai-sex-victims-relate-tales-of-duplicity-and-horror

https://www.state.gov/reports/2021-trafficking-in-persons-report/kuwait/

https://borgenproject.org/tag/human-trafficking-in-kuwait/

https://www.africanews.com/2016/04/25/young-zimbabwean-women-sold-into-sexual-slavery-in-kuwait//

https://www.youtube.com/watch?v=2IdII_n28e0&ab_channel=BBCNewsAfrica [an undercover exposure by BBC investigations on Kuwait's exploitation of maids]

https://futurism.com/human-traffickers-selling-slaves-instagram

https://www.sentinelassam.com/north-east-india-news/assam-news/assam-woman-sold-by-husband-in-kuwait-for-rs-2-lakh-returns-after-two-years-560600

https://www.globalsistersreport.org/news/people/lied-and-abused-trafficked-persons-zimbabwe-find-some-healing

https://www.youtube.com/watch?v=70m1YVZEYNA [Kuwait is hell]

https://www.undertoldstories.org/2017/06/20/how-human-traffickers-trap-women-into-domestic-servitude/

Africa

https://www.unodc.org/nigeria/en/human-trafficking-in-west-africa_-three-out-of-four-victims-are-children-says-unodc-report.html

https://borgenproject.org/human-trafficking-in-africa/

https://www.cambridge.org/core/books/african-court-of-justice-and-human-and-peoples-rights-in-context/human-trafficking-in-africa/9CDA6F771919FB283583F5C4196678B0

https://www.state.gov/reports/2021-trafficking-in-persons-report/south-africa/

https://www.youtube.com/watch?v=miH2IZXhZ1c

https://www.youtube.com/watch?v=aEBM6oX-4yg

https://www.africanews.com/2016/04/25/young-zimbabwean-women-sold-into-sexual-slavery-in-kuwait//

Latin Americas

https://www.youtube.com/watch?v=UliBqg5D6qw&ab_channel=ThomsonReutersFoundation

https://www.youtube.com/watch?v=vwh6VSyiE9A

https://www.voanews.com/a/episode_venezuelan-migrants-being-trafficked-colombian-border-officials-warn-4545821/6114345.html

https://www.state.gov/reports/2021-trafficking-in-persons-report/brazil/

https://www.upworthy.com/very-disgusting-not-sexy-things-are-happening-on-the-streets-of-brazil

https://www.unodc.org/unodc/en/human-trafficking/Webstories2021/main-drivers-of-human-trafficking-in-brazil.html

https://www.youtube.com/watch?v=VdaKma5giC4&ab_channel=Escravo%2CNemPensar%21

https://www.youtube.com/watch?v=yEUt-5B9-Pk&ab_channel=StanfordGlobalStudies

https://www.state.gov/reports/2021-trafficking-in-persons-report/venezuela/

https://insightcrime.org/news/venezuela-other-plight-sex-trafficking-trinidad-and-tobago/

https://www.connectas.org/sexual-trafficking-guyana-venezuela/

https://orato.world/2021/08/30/venezuelan-fled-from-human-traffickers-victims-in-the-bahamas/

https://theexodusroad.com/human-trafficking-in-colombia/

Europe

https://www.swedenabroad.se/es/embajada/netherlands-the-hague/current/calendar/how-do-we-combat-trafficking-in-human-beings-for-the-purpose-of-sexual-exploitation/

https://www.youtube.com/watch?v=2phCYhsp43Y

https://borgenproject.org/human-trafficking-in-the-netherlands/

https://www.state.gov/reports/2021-trafficking-in-persons-report/netherlands/

https://www.state.gov/reports/2021-trafficking-in-persons-report/italy/

https://borgenproject.org/human-trafficking-in-italy/

https://www.dw.com/en/trafficking-women-in-europe-the-nigerian-mafia-in-italy/av-58714558

https://www.youtube.com/watch?v=7pMmuEjugJ8

https://freedomcollaborative.org/webinar-library/sex-work-migration-exploitation-and-trafficking-in-europe

https://www.friendsofeurope.org/events/interrupted-journeys-the-human-cost-of-trafficking/

UK, Australia, New Zealand, China

https://www.nationalcrimeagency.gov.uk/news/38-arrested-as-national-law-enforcement-drive-targets-child-traffickers

https://www.humanrightspulse.com/mastercontentblog/taking-a-closer-look-into-the-uks-human-trafficking-crisis

https://www.state.gov/reports/2021-trafficking-in-persons-report/australia/

https://en.wikipedia.org/wiki/Human_trafficking_in_Australia

https://www.state.gov/reports/2021-trafficking-in-persons-report/new-zealand/

https://www.rnz.co.nz/news/national/446092/new-zealand-not-doing-enough-to-stop-trafficking-us-report-says

https://www.sixthtone.com/news/1009813/chinas-human-trafficking-problem-goes-far-beyond-the-chained-woman

https://www.state.gov/reports/2021-trafficking-in-persons-report/china/

Are you stirred up? Are you feeling fired to help in some way or the other? I suggest you keep that fire burning and let it not lose fuel. You can make use of it to reflect light. Let it spread worldwide to light up the darkness of trafficking whether you are in the US, UK, Canada, Europe, Middle East, Australia, India, Thailand,

Philippines, Nigeria….wherever. Get in contact with the foundations, health care, corporate, government, or non profits [NGOs].you may also start a new organization! Your efforts will help areas of:

- Investigations

- Rescue

- Law enforcement and border security

- Legal advocacy

- Judicial procedures and convictions

- Shelter

- Rehabilitate, repatriate and reunite

- Medical treatment

- Psychological therapy and counseling

- Education, teaching new skills and job placements

- Renew positive changes in the lives of the captivated and survivors

Please encourage others to read and share this book. Partnership to translate, reprint and publish is welcome. Please find my contact details on 'About the author page'

Since the renewal of FCRA in India has affected small time foundations and independent activists, you may donate to:

Manohar P. Waghela
State Bank of India
Branch: Mira Bhayander Road
Account: 32471931865
IFSC code SBIN0011695

Raju Baman
State Bank of India
Branch: MAL BAJAR
Account: 33010479564
IFSC code SBIN0002084

Neither do people light a lamp and put it under a bowl. Instead they put it on its stand, and it gives light to everyone in the house. In the same way, let your light shine before others, that they may see your good deeds and glorify the Almighty God in Heaven - Matthew 5:15-16, The Holy Bible

About the Author

Jeffson Nathan has travelled and lived in various parts of the world and in India. With a background of hospitality, Christian ministries and US diplomatic mission security, he has served a few years in the areas of surveillance, investigations and senior police liaisons for Anti Sex Trafficking in Mumbai, India. He has been part of some effective rescues of victims and conviction of traffickers. He is a social media influencer and is known for edification.

Besides the next proposed book on Religious Freedom, he has authored the following Christian and secular books in the past now available on Amazon:

- It's a Wake Up Call from worldly influences
- Victory over Adversity
- Break Free from Stigmas of Common Mental Disorders